Beca...
Life...

Gift

Because Life is a *Gift*

Disha

Srishti
PUBLISHERS & DISTRIBUTORS

Srishti Publishers & Distributors
N-16, C. R. Park
New Delhi 110 019
editorial@srishtipublishers.com

First published by
Srishti Publishers & Distributors in 2014

Copyright © Disha, 2014

10 9 8 7 6 5

The author assert the moral right to be identified as the author of this work.

Disclaimer: This is a work of non-fiction. All the stories in this book have been narrated to the author by the person concerned and have been reproduced herein with their due permission. The author has attempted to verify most facts through publicly available information to a certain extent, otherwise relying on the version narrated to her.

Printed and bound in India

*I am dedicating this book to my mother who has always
been my best friend, biggest support and whose
never-say-die spirit and moral values have
made me what I am today.*

*I am grateful to God for blessing me with such a
loving and caring family.*

Contents

Acknowledgements

No accomplishment, however big or small, is possible without the support of one's family, friends and the Almighty. This book may have been authored by me, but could not have been possible without the support of many people.

My family has always been special to me, always encouraging me to chase my dreams. My mother and mamaji have been the biggest inspirations in my life.

Thanks to all my friends, fans, readers and critics for showering me with so much love and affection for my first book My Beloved's MBA Plans. Each review and email that came to me mattered. Frankly, I had never thought I would pen down another one, but your support and encouragement made it happen. I look forward to hearing from all of you again.

Special thanks to the families and friends of people who have been covered in the book for opening their hearts and sharing their lives' good and bad moments with me.

And finally, each time I was stuck with my words or faced any kind of dilemma, my faith and belief in God helped me go the extra mile. Thank you, God.

Introduction

Graduating on that day were five hundred of us. Each one of us was excited to be receiving the degree for which we had burnt the midnight oil. Parents, friends, and spouses were present to be a part of this important milestone – the graduation ceremony of the Indian Institute of Management, Calcutta.

As our friends went on stage, we clapped hard. But how could one go on clapping for five hundred people? The applause started to fade in the middle of the ceremony. And then a young boy came on stage. Suddenly, the entire hall stood up to celebrate his joy, salute his determination and respect his journey. It was on that day that I met Suresh. It was at that moment that the concept of this book was born.

Suresh is among the first few hundred percent visually impaired persons to graduate from the prestigious Indian Institute of Managements, and the first one to do so from Calcutta. Every year, close to two lakh candidates compete to get into the IIMs. Less than four thousand actually make it. It was no ordinary feat that a blind boy had not just been able to get admission, but was today graduating along with so many 'abled' people. The fact that Suresh was amongst us was a moment of enlightenment for me. Till that day, I had looked at a differently-abled person with sympathy. But Suresh's determination made me abashed of my thoughts. It was not about Suresh's limitation but my own, the fact that I had never looked beyond the disability of a handicapped person, leave aside thinking of his or her bright future. Suresh showed me that if someone really wants to achieve something in life, he or she finds a way.

The more I researched about disabilities the more I realised how wrong I was. That so many things I had believed all my life were nothing more than myths and wrong notions I had imbibed from the society. Never before had I seen a visually impaired person on the road and felt that he was worthy of respect. Never before had I imagined a physically or mentally disabled person to be capable of achieving something extraordinary. Never before had I looked beyond a person's disability and seen him as more than a differently-abled person.

As the myths dispelled, there were a lot of questions. In a county where 2.1% of our population is disabled, why is it that almost all major public places are still not accessible? Why is it that we still do not see them sitting next to us in our offices, working as our colleagues? Why is it that people like Suresh are confined to their homes, made to curse their destinies and pitied upon? Biases like these have plagued the lives of millions of disabled people across the world. People have looked down upon them. Governments have failed to provide them infrastructural support. Societies have written them off.

Fortunately, few such people have managed to rise above all this to conquer the same world. To take their destinies in their hands and prove the world wrong. They have proven how disability is not a curse; it is only a different way of living. This book resulted out of my interactions with these people and my sheer appreciation for those who have the guts to take the risk and follow their dreams, despite the roadblocks and negative attitude of the society towards them.

In this book, there are 15 real life stories of differently-abled people – their lives, struggles and victories. At first glance, the book might seem to be relevant only for someone who is either going through a similar phase in life or has a close friend/relative/family member who is differently-abled. But far from it, the book is as much for all those who have no connection whatsoever to any disability. These stories are not just about disabilities. These are about the triumph of spirit, about the power of will, and about the determination of the human soul.

As you read the book, slow down to not just read the written words but also feel and live the angst, struggles, hopes, dreams, and strengths of the characters in these stories between the lines. Each story carries the message – 'nothing is impossible'.

Writing this book has made me a better human being. The journey has been enlightening, humbling. I hope the readers too will learn a lot through the people of the book and the book will leave everyone enriched.

Disabled or Differently-abled

There is a constant dilemma and debate both within and outside the disabled community where the term 'disabled' itself brings in a lot of negative connotation with it. Because by labelling someone as disabled, we are assuming right away that the person is incapable. A lot of handicapped people often take offence when the society at large uses this word to address them. The term '**differently-abled**' was first proposed (in the 1980s) as an alternative to **disabled**, **handicapped**, etc., on the grounds that it gave a more positive message and so avoided discrimination towards people with disabilities. They preferred to be called 'differently-abled' because, if for example, on the one hand, one was visually impaired, on the other hand, one also had a developed sensory capability. Even if one was wheelchair-bound, there were no limitations to his/her imaginative thinking, creative abilities and ingenuity.

While both these thought processes are worthy of respect and consideration, I personally feel it is not either-or but a combination. To me, the fact of the matter is that a wheelchair-bound person cannot move around with as much freedom, and the hearing impaired cannot hear what people around him are discussing. At the same time, though there are limitations, those can be conquered by other extraordinary capabilities of such people.

In this book, I have used both the terms in conjunction without limiting my thoughts or biasing my opinion for either.

Sai Prasad Vishwanathan: Celebrate Life Dreaming, Hoping and Believing

Disability is not what you are born with;
It is what you choose to be.
Life is a journey with many roadblocks;
While you are here, make the most of it.

When a young boy is thrown out of school because he has special medical needs, does he ever think of graduating one day from one of the leading B-schools of the world – the Indian School of Business? When he finds it difficult to move around in his home and fears the staircase, can he dream of going alone to a new country? When life confines the same boy to a wheelchair, can he ever think of skydiving from 14,000 feet? Do his dreams remain buried in a dark corner of his heart or does he dare himself to fulfil them?

Sai has not just shaken my deep-rooted stereotypes and myths about disability, he has also proven that come what may, every individual can either be a master or a slave of his fate depending on the choices he makes for himself. A change maker, recipient of many prestigious awards and honours, an ISB alumnus,

While driving a scooter was his first stint with freedom of movement, Sai spread wings when he tried his hand at skydiving. He holds a Master's degree from a foreign university and works to create awareness for the differently-abled, for which he has been felicitated at various occasions.

Sai Prasad's indomitable spirit and self-belief has caught on the imagination of the entire world. Sai is a torchbearer in the darkness, a ray of hope in the lives of the hopeless. For no matter how hard the times are, Sai refuses to accept defeat. Through 'Sahasra', he wishes to touch the lives of many others like him.

This is the story of the unstoppable 'yuva', story of Sai Prasad Vishwanathan.

Sai Prasad was born in Tamil Nadu in the year 1984. Owing to an extraneous growth in his spinal cord, Sai had to be operated upon when he was just thirteen days old. Due to the carelessness of the doctors, the lower half of his body was left dysfunctional during this surgery. The child was left wheelchair-bound for the rest of his life.

Where there were to be celebrations, there was an eerie silence for Sai's family. For a young girl, motherhood is the happiest phase of her life. But for Sai's mother, it meant a team of doctors explaining medical jargon to her, telling that her new born child would not be able to sense anything in the lower half of his body. As if this was not enough, everyone around her tried to discourage her about the future of such a child and the futility of raising him.

But come what may, Sai's parents were determined to bring up their child as any other parent would. They firmly resolved not to be bothered by the attitude of the society and instead decided to move to Hyderabad – a new place where no one knew them and where they did not have to deal with sympathy and pity.

From day one, Sai's father wanted to keep Sai away from the shadow of people who pitied him. He sincerely felt that there were some problems which could not be solved collectively. The family would do better on its own. In any case, exposing Sai to so much of negativity was not going to solve any problem but would only lead to more dejection. In a new city, among strangers, the family began life anew with a differently-abled child.

However, that was just the beginning of the struggle. Sai's illness was progressive. While his parents admitted him to a school, Sai's condition deteriorated. He found it difficult to even go to the washroom and was often unable to control his bladder and bowel movements. The parents of other children objected to his studying along with their children. They were worried about a possible spread of infection in the class.

Sai was an academically brilliant child, so the school wanted to retain the bright lad. But when the school authorities feared backlash from other parents, they eventually asked Sai's parents to move him to another school. In the next three years, Sai changed three schools.

Each time he got admission in a new school, it took him time to adjust to the new environment and the new people around him. But soon the same old pattern of other parents' complaints would emerge, and by the end of every year, the school would drop Sai off the student list.

In all those years, family support was extremely important. Amidst changing schools and adjusting to new environments, the only constant thing for the child was his parent's undying and selfless love. No matter what happened at school, the pampering and love at home compensated for everything for little Sai. His parents would keep instilling confidence in him, making sure he never felt inferior to anyone. His father would plan his study routines, read out motivational stories to him and keep him occupied. Amidst all the household chores, his mother would drop and pick him up from school every day and help him with his daily activities. Had it not been for the selfless love and commitment of his parents, Sai would probably not have been what he is today.

During the course of my research for the book, I came across many parents who keep their child confined to their homes for the fear of the unknown. By doing this, they are not just being unjust to their child but are also reinforcing the wrong beliefs that disabled people are not capable enough. By bringing up Sai in such an unconventional, loving and bold manner, Sai's parents have indeed set a great example for society to follow.

Sai realised that if he was to succeed, he had to outshine in academics. That would help him compensate for everything else. From then on, Sai started topping his class year after year. This changed the school's attitude towards him. It did not want to let go of a topper student. No longer did Sai need to change schools. Sai too resolved to care less for what the world thought of him. He started sitting separately in the class and focussing just on his books and studies.

As Sai started getting excellent grades, other students started befriending him. For the first time, his batchmates started recognising him for his capability rather than his disability. For the first time, people started noticing him for the right reasons and or the first time, sympathy turned into respect.

Just when it seemed things seemed to be finally falling into place for Sai, another accident turned the tide of his life for the worse.

He stepped on an iron nail and it lodged into his left foot. But since he had no sensation in the foot, he did not feel any pain and kept moving around in school unaware. It was only when he came home that his mother noticed blood and the nail and immediately rushed him to the nearest doctor. The nail was taken out but the septic wound had left him more handicapped. In his medical state, a wound takes a long time to heal. For him, it never did.

No amount of medication helped. Sai's whole foot developed infection and the same spread throughout his body. Sai had recurrent fever and was completely confined to a wheelchair. Until then, Sai could walk, though with difficulty. But this accident left the boy completely crippled for life. And yet his spirit refused to accept defeat. Each difficult situation made him even more determined to take things head on.

> *"Years after you are gone, people will not remember you for what obstacles you faced. People will remember how you emerged victorious."*

Sai received the Pratibha Scholarship and gold medal from the Chief Minister of Andhra Pradesh for his brilliant academic performance in high school. In the year 2002, Sai got into Electrical Engineering at the Chaitanya Bharathi Institute of Technology. Even though the college was just five kilometres away from his home, it was not easy for Sai to commute.

His mother would drive him to college and back home every day. But it was becoming increasingly difficult for her to do so as she had to take care of everything at home too. That was when Sai decided to learn driving a scooter. This gave him his first taste of freedom.

> *"I still remember how elated I was. For the first time, I could be on my own. It was a milestone. My college administration too was extremely helpful and made extraordinary efforts to ensure I could manage as much on my own."*

Sai's academic brilliance continued and he topped every exam. With a supportive environment, Sai began to think the sky was the limit for him. He dreamt of getting into the National Thermal Power Corporation (NTPC), a Maharatna PSU, post the completion of his engineering. But the journey of life had never been easy on him.

It was during an industrial visit to the NTPC that Sai first came face to face with the reality of a difficult future ahead for him. NTPC's plant was not at all accessible for a person with a disability. What had been a dream company for him to get into after his graduation was now a distant dream. Despite all his merits and capabilities, he wondered how he could work there when he found it difficult to move around even for a day? Even if he could somehow manage, would they even consider him for the job, no matter how excellent his academic performance had been? At that moment, his future seemed uncertain. For the first time, Sai was scared he might never find a suitable job despite his brilliance. He decided he would forget all his career plans and dream companies. Instead, he would apply to each and every company that would come for campus placements. Like every child, he too had dreamt of becoming the bread earner for his family. Thus, getting a job became a matter of necessity rather than a choice.

Sai discussed his apprehensions with the college authorities. He wanted to be interviewed impartially and reveal his handicap only after the interview. The college understood his predicament and when Infosys came to the campus for recruitment, the college placement committee purposefully kept Sai's interview post lunch. When the interviewers had gone out for lunch, Sai was sneaked into the interview room so he could be seated before they came in. They did not see his disability until the very end when his interview got over and he turned to go out of the room. By then, Sai had already left a wonderful impression on the interviewers and was selected.

The new joinees at Infosys undergo induction training at their Mysore campus. His parents were scared of letting him go anywhere outside Hyderabad. Despite multiple requests to Infosys, it did not agree to his skipping the Mysore training. Instead, it promised him the best of infrastructure to make his stay comfortable. Sai's parents were skeptical though, understandably. But seeing him reluctant to give up on the only job opportunity he had, they relented. Sai moved to the Mysore campus. And all his doubts were put to rest once he reached there. Infosys turned to be the biggest turning point in Sai's life.

Infosys campus actually made him feel independent for the first time in his life. The Infosys campus was easily so accessible and Sai needed no help whatsoever to move around. It was a big revelation to him that life could be so much better, if only the infrastructure was good. Sai wished he would never have to leave that place. A new word was added to his dictionary: 'accessibility'.

Back in Hyderabad after the training, Sai started researching more about accessibility. It was then that he first learnt how the infrastructure abroad helped many differently-abled people lead a life of dignity and independence. Awareness about the same sowed in him a longing to go abroad.

Sai felt that Infosys in all likelihood would never send him abroad on any assignment. Thus the only option for him to go abroad was if he were to go to study further. Sai applied to various universities for his Master's in engineering. He received a research scholarship to attend the University of Wisconsin.

Little did he realise that even though he was learning to be independent, the people around him, especially his parents, still felt he could not manage on his own. They had not seen the difference right infrastructure had brought in their child's life and were thus hesitant. It took Sai a lot of counselling sessions where he made his parents talk to the university council and showed them the facilities abroad over internet to finally convince them.

Away from his family, in a land that had the coldest winters of the world, Sai not just survived, but thrived. He found that the needs of the disabled were kept in mind in all places, from the airport to the public buses, right from the classrooms to his hostel.

"It perturbed me that in India, instead of being helped, the disabled are told that their condition is due to sins and 'karmas' of their past life. There are people like me in India who are not even aware of how the quality of their lives could be transformed just by better facilities."

Sai wanted to create awareness about the importance of disabled-friendly infrastructure. He created videos showcasing the infrastructure in US. But those did not gather much attention. That is when he decided he needed to do something different, something that would make the world sit up and notice.

In 2008, Sai took to the skies and decided to skydive from 14,000 feet; a feat which even perfectly normal people hesitate to try. For Sai, the challenge was not in taking off, but in landing. How could Sai land on his feet? His feet would have to be tied and he would have to land on his back with sufficient cushioning to avoid any accident. Easier said than done! Was the risk worth taking? What if he failed?

Sai demonstrated that given the right opportunity and support, even a child for whom the mere act of getting on a bus, climbing stairs, or reaching school without support was a challenge, could do wonders.

This time, his voice was noticed. Being the first disabled Indian to skydive from 14,000 feet, Sai's name was entered in the

Limca Book of Records. Suddenly people realised that if the right infrastructure was provided, there were no unchartered territories that a differently-abled person could not venture into. The Ability Foundation in Chennai called him to India to honour him for his extraordinary achievement. Indian newspapers covered his daring feat extensively. Sai was heard; his mission accomplished. But the same was also a start of the next phase of his life.

During a talk at the CevinKare award ceremony, Sai met a lot of MBA graduates and discussed the opportunities back home. This meeting convinced him to come back to India and to contribute to his country's growth. He applied to the Indian School of Business for its flagship PGP programme.

The minimum experience required for ISB's PGP programme was two years. But Sai had only one year's experience. When he spoke to the admission council, they evaluated his profile and decided to consider his case as an exception. Post his interview, his application was accepted. Sai joined ISB in April 2010.

"To enter the gates of one of India's most coveted institutes as a student was a proud moment for me."

During the course of his studies, Sai was once invited by his school to share his experiences with the students and inspire them to dream big. So popular was Sai among his juniors that the school had to eventually charge a nominal fee of ₹100 to restrict the number of attendees. The money collected was used by the school to set up the first alumni scholarship for the needy. That is when Sai thought of converting it into a full-fledged social venture. He discussed the scalability of this option with one of his professors at ISB, who happened to be a consultant with the Ministry of Social Justice. The professor advised Sai to extend this workshop to the rural segment where there was lack of awareness of the whole concept of higher education. A new beginning was made and the venture was named the Sahasra Foundation.

Students in the Sahasra programme pay a nominal admission fee for the workshops, where along with practical information about career planning, Sai quotes several inspirational stories and leadership examples. Till date, more than 20,000 students have participated in the programme in various college and university campuses. Sahasra has generated more than $100,000. Sai has used the money in scholarships for needy students and has built a team of young leaders who pass the message to others. The workshops are held in the form of storytelling with the focus being not just on success stories but also on failures and the learning from it.

> "When I got into CBIT, I did not make it to the IITs or other top colleges. But life did not stop there. I decided to make the best use of whatever opportunities I had, rather than to create a fuss over my failures. The same was the story of my NTPC dream. I give similar practical messages through my workshops to the students. We create stories in which the central character is someone everyone can relate to in some way or the other."

Sai also works to encourage and promote employment for the poor as well as the physically challenged people in the country.

> "I want to promote employment for the physically challenged people. If you notice, there are lots of places where the disabled can be easily employed. For example, the job of a traffic policeman at the crossing is all about sign language. He does not need much communication in any other manner. However, the daily exposure to the noise and high

*decibel levels makes him prone to hypertension and stress.
Can we not employ a deaf person in that job? He would be
least bothered by the constant noise and be able to give his
best to the job. Similarly, at all those jobs where purely data
entry work is to be done, can we not employ people who
cannot hear or are confined to wheelchairs?"*

Sai has raised pertinent questions and is looking for answers
from all of us. In fact, Sai's thoughts reminded me of a beauty
parlour I had once visited where a girl was visually handicapped
but she was busy dressing up a bride. My first reaction was how
was it possible at all? But proper training and support had made
the girl adept at handling such clients at the parlour despite her
own impairment. I would have never believed it had I not seen it
with my own eyes.

There are close to 40,000 jobs where the disabled can be
fruitfully employed. In the recent past, we have seen big joints like
KFC employ visually impaired people. The question then is not
whether they can do it. The question is how we support them.

Sai's vision for changing the perceptions of society and the
corporates towards the disabled community, especially in the areas
of employment has been published in the Harvard Business Review
called 'The Solution Revolution'. Sai also works with a few NGOs
on guiding universities, in making their campus infrastructure
disabled-friendly.

On the day of his graduation from ISB, the university made all
efforts to make the stage accessible for him. They never let him feel
excluded. Sai wants to pass on the same baton to other universities
too.

Little gestures from institutional bodies can go a long way
in helping the differently-abled. Kudos to ISB for its sensitivity

towards the needs of the differently-abled. Kudos to Sai for not just appreciating these little things, but also endeavouring to pass these on so no one else faces the same hurdles that he had.

Of late, Sai has also worked for the cause of climate change and environment protection. So much so, that Robert Swan, the first person to walk across the North-South poles approached him. Sai was selected as one of the thirty members of the 2041 Antarctic Youth Ambassador Programme. The programme offers young leaders a chance to explore Antarctica and gain firsthand knowledge of the continent's fragile and changing ecosystem. What is even more significant is that in the twenty day expedition, he was the only differently-abled person in the entire team of eighty young men and women.

"I was excited and nervous, and wondered if I would be able to manage in the extreme weather conditions. But determination to enjoy life made me take the plunge."

In 2010, Sai received the Helen Keller Role Model Person of the Year award for his contributions towards society. This was followed by the ISB Torchbearer award. Sai's speeches have been very well received at prominent forums like the TEDx. He was also featured in the disability episode of India's popular TV programme *Satyamev Jayate*. The show, hosted by Aamir Khan, received tremendous response from all across the nation.

But the real success of Sai's life and of Sahasra transcends borders. Sahasra has been recognised as one of the top ten business plans submitted to the Global Social Venture Competition held by the University of California, Berkeley. Wharton and Kellogg have jointly released a report of Sahasra's work, promoting it as a sustainable scalable model for inclusive growth of society.

"This work is important to me because the value our work provides will remain in the hearts of many long after I am gone. I am happy if my efforts can touch some lives."

Sai has recently left his job at Deloitte as a technology risk consultant to pursue his entrepreneurial journey. More than anything else, Sai has shown the world what a person is capable of surmounting. From a person who could not move on his own to studying abroad and skydiving, Sai's enthusiasm and dedication towards Sahasra is indeed inspirational.

His thought process inspires many to think beyond the ordinary. His writings are a real inspiration and his determination and positive attitude oozes hope for the differently-abled community. Sai not just has a vision and a mission in life, but also concrete plans of how he will execute them. He wants to transform the nation's ideologies towards millions of their own countrymen.

Sai is one person who has touched my soul and will be my role model for years to come. Let not the fire die; ignite it so it can lighten the world around you. For life is all about choices and not what could have been.

Sai can be reached at happy.blissfull@gmail.com.

Hridayeshwar Singh Bhati: Checkmate Life!

I can brood on what life has offered;
And keep asking it 'why me'.
Or I can take charge of my fate;
And create my own destiny.

Each one of us is gifted in some way or the other. God has his own ways of creating checks and balances. As humans, we focus only on the negative side of life and that's what makes life difficult for us. But my outlook towards life changed after meeting this child prodigy who has emerged as a global inspiration and is in the true sense, a great milestone in the world of disability. A miracle boy, the youngest patent holder in the country, India's Stephen Hawking, are phrases associated with this genius.

He is indeed India's pride. What is even more amazing is the fact that the young master has achieved all that at an age of just ten years! My heart goes out to Hridayeshwar and I ask God why he cannot cure the young child. Hearty has proven that a disability may not be cured, but it can surely be defeated. For Hridayeshwar has conquered and checkmated life!

From designing the ramp to be fitted in his father's car to enable free movement for him to inventing chess for 12-60 players, Hearty has taken challenges head on. He is encouraged in his innovative efforts by friends, family, his school and various institutions.

I call up Mr Sarower Bhati, Hridayeshwar's father to ask for an interview. Mr Bhati is worried. Do I want to commercialise the disability of his son into profit for myself? What are my reasons of writing the book, he asks. It is only when I convince him of my intentions that he obliges and we begin the conversation.

Hearty or Hridayeshwar Singh Bhati was born in September 2002 in Jaipur. Hearty was four years old when his parents first noticed their child was having problems in climbing stairs. The child however never complained to his parents. When the problem lingered on and none of the home remedies they tried worked, they took him to an orthopaedic who diagnosed him with a muscular disorder. Doctors in the All India Institute of Medical Sciences confirmed that it was a case of Duchenne Muscular dystrophy. Muscular Dystrophy (MD) is a group of muscle diseases that weaken the musculoskeletal system and hamper locomotion of a person. It also affects the lungs and other important organs of the body. And unfortunately, it worsens as one grows old.

Hearty's parents were distraught and shaken. They consulted several doctors but each told them the disease was incurable. Any medicines the child would take would have its own side effects. As if that was not enough, they were also told that the problem would progressively worsen with age. They did not know whether they should tell Hearty about it. How could they gather courage to tell their child that soon he would not be able to walk, that soon he would be confined to a wheelchair, and soon he would become an object of sympathy?

However, Hearty was braver than his parents had thought. He could sense something was amiss. But more than his own health issues, he was bothered about his parents' sad faces. Many a time when he would suddenly fall while walking and see his parent's sad faces, he would try to get up on his own. He would never cry but instead, keep a big smile on his face telling his parents that it was all part of growing up.

As time progressed, his body movements restricted. His parents had to take the tough call of restricting his activities, telling him not to play outdoors, and sometimes even telling him not to walk when the problem aggravated. On the one hand, they were doing all they could to protect him from any injury. On the other hand, their hearts were bleeding.

Hearty too began to understand and accept his condition. But he never lost hope to live his life to the fullest. The biggest solace for his parents was that Hearty was always smiling. Hearty had a strong willpower and the more his physical strengths gave away, the stronger became his will to live joyfully. His positive attitude kept him going.

Hearty is a special child as his parents tell me,

"Often he would ask questions to which even we did not have the answers. He had a different way of approaching things. He would not look at what the problem was, but the opportunity it presented."

With time, the complications of the disorder increased. Hearty could no longer walk. His parents wanted to pull him out of mainstream school and enrol him into a special school. But Hearty would have none of it. He hated to be given any 'special' or different treatment. When asked how he would manage, Hearty told his father he would find his way or carve out one.

From then on was born a boy with an extraordinary innovative frame of mind. He took charge of his mobility requirements. He designed his own toilet seat, wheelchair and even his father's car to suit his locomotive needs. Whenever he would come across a hurdle, he would think of ways to get around it. This was just a glimpse of what was to come. Hearty would soon be well-known across the globe.

Hearty shares his thoughts,

"I was disturbed to see there were not many special customized wheelchairs available in India, leave aside my hometown, Jaipur. I researched on the internet and found out ways in which I could design one as per my needs.

"I did not want to be constrained at home. Till a certain age, my father would lift me in his arms and seat me in the car. But for how long could I be dependent on him? Surely that was not sustainable in the years to come. Since I did not move too much, my body was becoming heavy. So I requested my father to buy a car which had a ramp entry attached. But there again I was disappointed. There were none which catered to the special needs of a physically challenged person. One day I asked my father to test drive a few cars and then finalised on the Eeco which had the capability to have a ramp attached. So when I would go to school, someone would attach the ramp to the car. I could get in the car without my father having to physically lift me. This made me feel much more independent. I researched more to even make the ramp attachment automated so I could move around freely."

What Hearty did was no simple feat given his age. His maturity and his refusal to be constrained by circumstances sets him apart. But the best thing about Hearty is that he never thinks just of himself when he innovates and invents. He told his parents to share his customised designs with other disabled people. What came out of his experiments was a low-cost wheelchair accessible mobility vehicle and a modified version of Maruti's Eeco car with a ramp attached for ease of access for the disabled community.

One of his dreams in life is to make the world disaster free. I was surprised to hear a ten-year-old child talk so maturely.

> *"What nature does is beyond our control. But disasters can be managed to curtail the damage they bring. Today we are building such tall buildings where an escape is impossible in case of even a simple fire. I wish to change that. I hope we become less greedy in our desire for globalisation. Hazards today will be disasters tomorrow, and disasters not only kill, but teach also. Disaster teaches us that a spark when neglected can burn down an entire house. The earth is not just a planet but our home and our existence tomorrow depends upon our preparations today. Let's not test the patience of Mother Nature too far. Instead, let us know her well and take care of her."*

His ideologies make me sit and think.

Hearty needs to get up at 5 am everyday because it takes him a while to get ready for school. When Hearty goes to school, a bottle is attached behind his chair into which he relieves his bladder. Else, he needs to be lifted by someone if he has to use the washroom. While sleeping, both his legs have to be supported at both ends of the bed. There are many hurdles to cross but the boy is cheerful and more alive than most of us. Hearty is mature and has a clear vision in life. With a heart of gold, Hearty is surely God's own child.

No wonder then that his parents feel having a child like Hearty has helped them become better human beings. His father tells us,

> *"Earlier, I would get angry often. But Hearty said something which changed me forever. He said, 'Anger is also a disability. I can't overcome my disability. You are lucky you can. Make an effort'."*

Who would have thought a ten-year-old child to even comprehend this deep a thought, leave alone expressing it in such a lucid manner? When people looked at him and sympathised, Hearty would tell his parents,

> *"I am a celebrity. That is why people are looking at me."*

Of course, at that time, he did not know he was to become one soon.

His fame and success came from another of his inventions coming out of his desire to play with his friends. Owing to his physical limitations, he could just play indoors. His friends would come home to play with him. One day he was playing chess with his father when four of his friends came and asked him if they could play along with them. His father dismissed their request saying chess was a game for only two players. But Hearty, being who he is, was not convinced. He searched on the internet for a chess game which could involve six players but could find none. The innocent child asked his father if they could design one together.

Looking into Hearty's eyes, his father instantly knew Hearty was serious.

Over the next few months, Hearty conceptualised the same. His father being a mathematics teacher helped him with the possible geometrical combinations possible for designing such a game. Initially, the duo thought that a hexagon would do. But then the cross over from the centre was troubling. At that point of time, Hearty rose to the occasion like a true inventor and remarked,

"Why not try a similar design on a circle?"

That was the moment circular chess was born. After months of research, Hearty had successfully designed chess for six players!

This magnificent achievement would have gone unnoticed and Hearty could have spent his life satisfied playing this new game with friends and family. But one of his friends' fathers, who also happened to be a newspaper editor, suggested that Hearty share his game with the world and file a patent for the same. Hearty was more than willing to share the game with others. Hearty's father filed for the patent in Hearty's name.

In a span of few months, Hearty caught the attention of the media and became a superstar. He was conferred several awards for his remarkable achievement. Media persons thronged his house to interview him, and deservingly so. After all, Hearty had just become India's youngest patent holder and the youngest disabled patent holder of the world. He was definitely the pride of the country.

Hearty has been invited to several conferences and has been presented with many awards. At one such press conference, Hearty promised to create a game of chess for sixty players. Asked what use a chess game of sixty players would have, he answered that we could have national as well as international chess championships and tournaments where several players from several countries could play concurrently. Club houses would make a lot of business with this game. He said that it could also be a boon in disguise for the disabled as well as for old people. Hearty said that chess was invented in India and is India's pride. It needed to be expanded by the medium of these innovative boards. Hearty's answer left the audience spellbound and speechless.

Hearty worked hard to make his dream a reality. Few months later, Hearty fulfilled his promise. He filed a patent for twelve and another for sixty players. The beauty of these innovative circular chess variants is that the rules are based on existing chess and the boards have more application and utility. He is a great child prodigy with three patents already to his name. I am sure he must be already thinking of his next invention.

Hearty also gives back to society in other ways. He teaches poor kids in his school. Whatever prize money he gets on winning competitions in school, he buys something for these kids.

As I listen to his deeds, I am humbled. How many of us, people with so many blessings in life, can think that way, leave aside do anything? But Hearty is God's own child and every action of his vouches for that. Hearty's parents, family, friends, and relatives are all proud of him. Delhi Public School, Jaipur gives him all the infrastructural support that he needs. Hearty on his part never let his problems become an excuse. I hope

Hearty's story becomes an inspiration not just for the disabled community but also makes mainstream schools become more acceptable, open and caring towards the disabled so that many more Heartys come forward.

Hearty has also encouraged his mother to take up a job. She says,

> *"I am a Ph.D. in English literature. Hearty tells me not to waste my education but share my knowledge with the world."*

Well aware of how technology can empower him and provide a better quality of life, Hearty is a gadget freak. His house is a technology store house. From the latest phone handset to X-BOX and Windows 8, Hearty loves to keep himself abreast of the latest happenings in the world of technology. He orders things from Flipkart and has a list of celebrities follow him on his Facebook page. Hearty wants to now convert his chess boards on an android platform. He wants to see people playing his game on X-box and play-stations.

Clearly, he is not disabled, but a specially-abled child. Clearly, he is living life each moment, and is an inspiration for everyone around the world. People are planning documentaries on him and filmmakers are queuing up to engage him in his summer vacations.

Hearty may have achieved all this. But for his parents, the fear always remains. From the time Hearty goes to school till the time he returns home, they are scared whether he has eaten well, whether he has had any difficulty; such thoughts constantly run through their minds. But the biggest worry is of Hearty's future, when they are not around anymore to care for him.

Questions and fears like these plague the parents of many such children. No one can replace the love and care of parents in one's life. And when one is confined and constrained by destiny, family support is the biggest factor which can keep one going. I hope the society comes together to extend a helping hand.

Hearty is lively and hopeful. He makes an attempt to not just overcome his own challenges, but to help others come out of theirs too. He touches my soul when he quotes a line he has written,

> *"The only disability is no self-esteem. People who cannot walk can fly with their attitude."*

He adds,

> *"I cannot walk but I am flying today."*

As the day progresses, I watch him go about his routine. Towards the evening, Hearty is tired and his friends come over. We decide to let the kids play and finish the interview. Hearty's father says,

> *"We just hope that each person reading this story prays for our son and someone's prayers are answered. Miracles can happen and we are hopeful."*

We sincerely hope somewhere, somehow a miracle happens and Hearty gets the best of the world. Hearty has taught me an important lesson – it's the quality of life and not the days spent on earth which matter.

Hridayeshwar can be contacted @ hridayeshwarbhati@gmail.com.

Disability and Education

Sai was forced to leave school after school. Hearty, on the other hand, found the best of infrastructural support in his alma mater. This raises an important question on the issues and importance of education in the context of differently-abled people.

About 70% of the differently-abled people in India have never been enrolled in schools. Of the remaining 30%, only 9% finally complete their secondary and higher education. The Persons with Disability Act Bill, 1995 clearly states that the onus is on both the central and state governments to ensure all disabled people get free education till the age of 18. The scheme of integrated education for disabled children was launched in 1974 to provide 100% financial assistance for fees, books, stationery, uniforms, travel allowances, escorts allowances for the severely handicapped, and boarding and lodging charges for those residing in hostels. But unfortunately, all such legislations have remained merely on paper. Not much attention has been paid to their implementation. Laws are conveniently made and forgotten.

Lack of accessible schools, refusal of many schools to even admit such children, lack of training of teachers to handle these children, a rigid curriculum and vague methods of evaluation are big deterrents for the education of differently-abled children.

I have also come across parents who have objected to their 'normal' child studying with a 'disabled' child. I often wonder what values are these parents inculcating in their own children with this kind of attitude. Which is a bigger deterrent – the incapability of the differently-abled children or the insensitivity of the society towards them?

There is an ongoing debate on whether differently-abled children should be sent to special schools or efforts should be made to include them in 'mainstream' education. My vote goes to the latter. How else will these children ever be a part of the same society? How will people like you and me interact with these children in our day-to-day lives and appreciate them as one amongst us? Unfortunately, there seems to be a long road ahead given that the coverage in mainstream schools as of date is less than 5%.

Many have said that such children are not capable of being part of mainstream schools and deserve special attention. But the little research I have done on the subject has proven that we do not need special schools, but more flexibility in our teaching pedagogy. With advancement in technology, things can be made much simpler and easier. A visually impaired child can learn if his books are Braille compatible. With software like JAWS, all study material can be fed into computers and taught. A hearing impaired child needs a sign language interpreter to be able to complete his education. A physically challenged person does not need reservation or quotas in schools, but more accessible school buildings. The need to focus on more skill-based higher education and training for differently-abled people to align them towards mainstream job opportunities is crucial. The educational system, especially higher education, needs to be more flexible and job-oriented for the differently-abled. The question is whether we really want to make a difference.

If the aim is to sincerely integrate the disabled with society, the first step would have to be through educational institutions. The question then is not why, but how.

Vinod Rawat:
Beyond the Odds

A storm came and took away my happiness;
A blessing came and gave me a second chance.
I cried over the storm and embraced the blessing.
To the tune of life, I blissfully dance.

In the first instant, Vinod looks like any other person in the crowd. You fail to notice his disability. When I speak to him for the first time, I feel as though I have known him for years. The warmth of his voice can easily touch a million hearts. Beyond the smile, I discover a man of strong will; a man whose story carries pain and leaves me disturbed for many days to come. Living a life supported on crutches for twenty-two years can make anyone lose the desire to enjoy life. His story is a story of the many street kids we see every day, but seldom stop to think about.

Vinod has gone beyond all odds to make his existence truly meaningful and inspiring. Vinod's physical disability has been no obstacle for him to conquer his dreams. From MTV to Ladakh, the journey has been truly magical.

Fighting poverty, fighting society, fighting drugs, fighting disability; this man has risen beyond the odds. Vinod has proven how some people's spirits can never be crushed. His journey

While riding a bike gave Vinod freedom, riding it up to Ladakh with a prosthetic limb was one of his rare feats. His calibre and never say die spirit has been applauded by various organisations and eminent personalities, including Rannvijay Singh of television show MTV Roadies, in which Vinod was a contestant.

shows that when time are tough, you will sail through it and live to see better days. Most importantly, it shows how we cannot deal with our inner demons by denying their existence, but by acknowledging and challenging them. Vinod's story is not special because of what he has achieved today. It is special because few have the courage to share their failures with such frankness and honesty; because it is in the darkest hours of life that a man's strength of character is truly tested.

Vinod Rawat was six years old when he was hit by a truck. One of his legs was badly hurt. The doctors estimated the expenses of ₹25,000 for his treatment. Vinod's family was in complete financial distress and could not arrange the money. Ultimately, the delay in the treatment cost Vinod one of his limbs. When the money was finally arranged, it was too late. After undergoing six operations in six months, Vinod lost his leg.

> "आस पास सब लोग ठीक हो कर चले जाते थे, पर मैं वहीं था।"
> *(I saw people around me getting well and returning home.*
> *But nothing changed for me.)*

Owing to multiple operations, his leg was rendered unfit for a standard artificial limb to be fitted. That's when the real struggle began for Vinod. He was the eldest son of the family. From being seen as an asset, he began to be seen as a liability.

As if that was not enough, he was ostracized by his own friends. In school, his friends would call him names, mock him, and snatch away his crutches. He would see children playing and wanted to play as well. But more than his physical disability, it was people's attitude that scared him. He craved for acceptance. At one point of time, he started seeing himself as a useless person and lost all interest in studies. He became dejected, left home and started sleeping on the streets. He started selling knives to earn his living. And that is when he fell into bad company. He started indulging in violence and drugs. He even had to go to jail a few times.

"Those were the darkest days of my life. All I felt was hatred, jealousy and anger."

As Vinod tells me his story, my eyes become moist. I dread to think how scarring these experiences must have been for a young child. I wonder how Vinod came out of it all to be what he is today.

As they say, every sunset is followed by a sunrise, a new beginning. Somewhere within Vinod, his conscience prompted him, pricked him to reform himself. Vinod wanted to get out of the bad company he had gotten into. But he found no hope. There was nothing for him to look forward to. It is easy to be swayed towards the wrong path, but difficult to get back on the right track.

However, where there is a will, there is a way. When you cannot help yourself, trust God. He helps you sail through difficult times. For Vinod, God came in the form of a stranger. And ever since then, Vinod has never looked back. What follows from here is nothing short of a miracle.

It was an evening in the year 1994. Vinod was sleeping on the streets when a man walked up to him and started talking to him. He told Vinod,

"Jesus loves you. Please stop all your bad acts."

Vinod retorted and asked,

"When I am going through troubled times, where is Jesus?
If Jesus does exist, why does he not take me out of this hell?
I want to live a good life. If I stay on the streets, either I will
kill someone or get killed."

Vinod had been strong enough to accept his shortcomings
and confess them to a stranger. The stranger was the much needed
angel in his life. He promised Vinod that he would soon come back
to help Vinod. Almost like a God-sent messenger.

Days later, the person returned. True to his words, he took
Vinod to a rehabilitation centre run by Christian Missionaries
called Bombay Teen Challenge where disabled street kids, drug
addicts, and rag pickers were brought and rehabilitated. Initially
uncomfortable living with these children, Vinod soon developed
a liking for the place. The disciplined environment taught him
to control his anger. Slowly, his smile returned and he learnt self
control.

"I realised how often we place our sense of self-worth upon
the way others treat us. I started wondering why was it that
I bothered about people who didn't care for me and in the
process, hurt those who did."

Initially Vinod was given the task of cleaning the rehab centre.
Subsequently, the director of the centre noticed the spark in Vinod's
eyes and got him admitted to a nearby night school. During the
day, Vinod would work at the centre. At night, he would go to the
school.

" जिन्दगी से चाकू छूरी निकल गए और *piano, guitar* आ
गए।"

[All the knives (bad habits) were gone and were replaced by a piano and guitar (good habits).]

"Life was full of melodies now. I had left behind all the violence."

Being a Christian missionary, the rehab centre also inculcated in him the habit of reading the Bible. Vinod would often reach out to children of prostitutes and read out the Bible to them. He would try to share his experiences with them, to inspire them to lead a good life and not fall into bad company. Life was returning back on track for Vinod when suddenly a bad news derailed everything. His father had passed away.

All of a sudden, the responsibility of his entire family fell on his shoulders. He had four sisters and two brothers. Vinod dropped out of school and began working part time in McDonalds. In the morning, he worked in the rehab centre, and in the evening in McDonalds. Whatever he earned, he gave it to his mother to run the household.

Vinod's story brings tears to my eyes. Life can be really harsh. A myriad of emotions run through my heart and I try my best to hold on to my emotions as Vinod continues his story.

Till 1997, Vinod still did not have an artificial limb. He had lost hope of ever getting one. Until one day, someone told him of the Jaipur Foot. The Jaipur Foot, also known as the Jaipur Leg, is a rubber-based prosthetic leg for people with below-knee amputations. Bhagwan Mahavir Viklang Sahyata Samiti in Jaipur makes customised limbs for disabled people and also fits them free of charge.

Vinod visited the centre, where the doctors told him,

"We will try our best."

These words were not new to Vinod. Many other doctors had earlier shown the same hope and later told Vinod that his case was different and out of their 'scope'. This time, however, it was a life changing event for Vinod when the doctor gave him a positive response. The pace with which they did so is praise-worthy. In the morning, they took Vinod's exact measurements and fitted the limb the same evening.

" मैंने खुद को आईने में देखा और कहा, यहाँ से नयी शुरूआत करनी है।"
(I looked at myself in the mirror and said, 'it is from here that life begins anew and afresh'.)

That was the second turning point in Vinod's life. After spending twenty-two years on crutches, he was able to finally stand on his feet. With his crutches gone, Vinod found a new world. He found a new respect for himself in the society. He was able to lead a better life. From being called a handicapped guy, he came to be known as a handsome guy. He did things he always wanted to do. Motorbikes were his passion. He now rode one, went for mountaineering camps and even went swimming.

Here was a new Vinod no one had known – full of passion. Respecting his new found ambitions, the director of the rehab centre decided to send him for leadership training to Portugal.

"It was my first flight. I was on cloud nine; proud of myself. From sleeping on the streets, I was now on my own taking initiatives to help others. All thanks to the help provided to me, I could achieve all that I did. I hoped to help others in the same way a stranger had helped me that day. The way someone picked me up from the streets, I wanted to touch lives of other street kids."

After the training, Vinod took on greater responsibilities at the centre. Finally in 2005, Vinod decided to move out of the centre.

> *"I could now take on the world on my own and did not have to be dependent on the rehabilitation centre. They had done their job. It was time for me to do mine. There were many other Vinods out there who were probably needier than me. They should get their chance; for which I needed to move out."*

Vinod was jobless after he left the centre wondering what to do for a living. Luck seemed to favour him as one day while walking, Vinod saw a huge crowd on the road. The auditions for *MTV Roadies* were on. But Vinod at that time did not know what *MTV Roadies* was. What he did know was that there was a yellow bike on display and that was to be given to the winner of the event.

Vinod had always been fascinated with bikes. When he saw the bike, he told himself it would definitely be worth a try and joined the queue. After standing for almost three hours in the queue, someone came out and said that they could all go back as the auditions were over. Dejected, he turned back. As he was walking away, the cameraman came to him and said that he looked like Sachin Tendulkar. Vinod joked how it was the other way round and Sachin looked like him. Impressed by his confidence and witty reply, he asked Vinod to go inside and give his reference. Vinod took the audition and came home.

In the evening, Vinod got a call from VJ Anushka. She asked him if he had checked his email. Vinod had seen some professional riders who had come there for the audition and was thus not too hopeful. But her call was definitely encouraging. He told her,

"Why should I waste my time checking my email when VJ Anushka is calling me herself? Tell me where do I come for the next round."

On the show, Vinod did not tell Raghu and Rajeev, the hosts, about his disability until at one point when they mistakenly shouted at him for his peculiar way of riding a bike. He rode the bike in a different style because of the artificial limb. When he told the two about his artificial limb, they were shocked. When he told them his story, they asked him if he would run away if they called the police. Vinod told them,

"I was, but no longer am scared of the police. I have left my dark past far behind."

Despite his disability, Vinod did very well in the show. He was one of the last guys to be voted out. He was sad when he had to go home after coming so close. But as a gesture to honour his achievement in the show, Raghu gave me him the keys to the bike. Vinod was ecstatic.

Subsequently, Vinod did a few advertisements for MTV and one for *Dainik Bhaskar* with the captain of the Indian cricket team, MS Dhoni.

"Those days when I walked into the street, people recognised me and would come up to take my autograph."

It was in the same year that Vinod got married. He had met his wife during his visits to an NGO where she worked. After a couple of meetings, they fell in love and decided to get married. The girl asked Vinod to come and talk to her parents.

Her mother was furious. After all, her daughter was perfectly 'normal'. Why should her daughter marry a 'disabled' guy? Love meant nothing to her. It took a lot of convincing to finally get her to agree to the match.

In the meanwhile, Vinod applied to the Bullet Club, a club of passionate bikers. But he was rejected citing his disability. The club said they did not want to take a risk with a disabled person. This incident made Vinod even more sensitive to the needs of the disabled people. He realised that differently-abled people had dreams, but people seemed to have little faith in their abilities. He decided to do something about it and very soon formed his own bikers' club for disabled people.

The group toured several places on bikes. But the dream of going to Ladakh remained unfulfilled. In 2011, there was a cloud burst in Ladakh which destroyed the entire region. Seventy-one towns and villages were damaged, including the main town in the area, Leh. More than nine thousand people were affected by the event. Unlike other travellers who go to Ladakh as tourists, Vinod wanted to travel for a social cause. Vinod decided he would do a charity collection drive through a bike rally and try to gather funds for the flood victims. He wanted to rebuild the damaged houses in Ladakh.

Each house would cost approximately three lakhs. He approached many corporate houses for funding the rally but nobody was ready to believe that a disabled man would be able to travel to Ladakh on a bike. Everyone refused to support or be a part of Vinod's expedition.

A well known premium bike company initially agreed to sponsor the trip but later backed out. No one thought it was possible, but Vinod knew he had to do it. He sold his gold chain to fund the ride. Fortunately, an international NGO called Habitat for

Humanity came forward at the last minute and agreed to sponsor the initiative.

Getting a team of daring individuals who would accompany him turned out to be more difficult than anticipated. It is every biker's dream to go to Leh in Ladakh. But the journey is full of challenges. There are problems of low pressure, low temperature, and lack of basic facilities. Even the fittest of travellers find it tough to cope. So when he proposed the idea to his club members, not many came forward. Vinod had an initial team of five out of which only three ultimately went on the expedition. The story of how Vinod managed to convince Manoj Mehta, one of his co-bikers is an interesting one in itself. Vinod was visiting the Jaipur prosthetic limb centre to seek their suggestion and also in the hope of finding like-minded people. He met Manoj who had recently lost both his legs and had come to the centre for artificial limbs. As Manoj and Vinod were waiting for their turns at the centre, they began a conversation.

Manoj was a farmer. He told Vinod his life was finished. When Vinod tried to motivate him, Manoj rebuffed him saying that it was very easy to preach but only one who had been through such grave circumstances could understand and appreciate the pain. That was when Vinod shared his own life story with Manoj. Manoj realised Vinod was like him and could then understand the depth of his words.

Vinod asked him if he wanted to be a part of the Ladakh trip. Manoj first thought he was kidding. How could a man with no limbs even think of riding through such rugged terrain, leave aside actually doing it? Manoj found it difficult to even move around to earn his living and here was a crazy person asking him to come along to Ladakh. Vinod understood his dilemma and promised to extend his complete support and even train him for the same.

Manoj reluctantly agreed. Something in Vinod's eyes told Manoj that this could be his chance.

Vinod put his heart and soul in training Manoj for the next ten days.

> "For me, it was not just training someone to ride a bike with artificial limbs. More than the physical training, it meant overcoming the mental barriers – his fears and his agony. The spirit of fearlessness and determination triumphed. We triumphed."

Finally, the three bikers started their journey on 30 July 2011 from Mumbai. Along with Vinod and Manoj was Santosh Dhumal. Santosh had been affected by polio. The trio had to carry food, spare parts, clothes and air pump on their bikes. Each biker carried a load close to 110 kilos. The trip was full of adventure. One obstacle led to another, and Rohtang Pass turned out to be one of the deadliest places.

> "At the back of my mind, I always wondered how Manoj would manage. Our artificial limbs often got stuck in the snow. In my previous expeditions, I had seen many groups where there was no discipline among the riders. I wanted it to be different for my team. I set a rule. Whatever be the situation, if one bike breaks down, everyone stops.
>
> "Unity and trust were going to be our key strengths. I instructed my team that no matter whatever happened, we all needed to move together. If we succeed, we succeed together. If we fail, we also fail along with the others. And that is how we overcame all the roadblocks.

"After crossing Rohtang, we were filled with pride and honour."

The team finally reached Ladakh on 13 August 2011. In Ladakh, they travelled to the world's highest motorable pass Khardhung La.

"Our limbs froze and fingers were swollen. But our determination was firm."

When the team finally reached, they hoisted the Indian flag and sang the national anthem with the Army. Later, when the army men got to know of the team's daring spirit, the men in uniform saluted the team for its achievements.

With the help of the men in the Army, they got down to reconstructing houses in Ladakh. As a mark of tribute, on 15 August 2011 during the flag hoisting ceremony, the minister announced that Vinod would hoist the flag.

"वो मेरे लिए सबसे बड़ा सम्मान था, सबसे बड़ा मेडल।"
(That was the biggest honour, the biggest award for me.)

What a transition!

From someone who used to attack with knives to one who helped the devastated families start their lives afresh! It is as much about the chance that life gave him as about what he made out of it.

Speaking of medals, I ask Vinod about the awards he has received. He candidly replies,

"I have received a lot of awards. But after the ceremony, the same people who give the award, refuse to even recognise you."

Many corporate institutions give awards just so they can fulfil their CSR obligations. Such awards hold no significance either for the recipient or the giver. Awards hold no meaning if they are not given in the right spirit of respect. Disabled people do not need sympathy but respect.

Vinod has conquered several other mountain peaks since then. He has also been participating in the Mumbai marathon for the last eleven years. Several high profile people meet him in the rally and promise him support. But all is forgotten once the marathon is over.

Vinod is currently working in an event management company. The organisation works towards conducting motivational workshops for inspiring people for a healthy and good living. Vinod has delivered several motivational speeches and has conducted counselling sessions to help people come out of distressful situations.

"My motto in life is that wherever I go, whenever people meet me, I should make them feel good about life and make them realize that it is worth living to the fullest."

Rising from the streets, fighting poverty and finally his disability, Vinod has risen from the ashes; a man whose story deserves applause, whose strength deserves respect. Surely, if there is pain in life, there is healing too. If there is hopelessness, there is hope too. If there is ugliness, there is beauty too. The idea is to never give up on the gift called 'life'.

Vinod can be contacted at vinodrawat301@gmail.com.

Disability and Parenting

Parents – "you are the bows from which your children as living arrows are sent forth," said Kahlil Gibran.

Much of what we are is an outcome of the values instilled in us by our parents. It is at home that we first learn to speak and it is our parents who help us take our first step. It is at home that our character is shaped. The value of parenting in our lives cannot be over-emphasised.

And in the lives of a person with disability, the family, especially parents, play the most important role. When a disabled person faces criticism, negativity, social and infrastructural barriers every day, the atmosphere at home either motivates him to keep going or pulls him down further. While few people in this book craved for family love and spent a major part of their childhood among strangers, many others had parents who stood rock solid behind their children, reminding their child that he was special, differently-abled and not disabled.

Sai's parents made a conscious choice of moving to a different city to bring up their child away from the baggage of negativity. Hearty's father is less a father, more of a friend to the young boy. George's and Suresh's parents believed in their child's dreams and dared to look beyond the limitations of visual impairment.

During my research for the book, I also met parents who felt all was lost for their disabled child. They refused to send their child to a school and refused to talk of a future for their child. Though a lot many parents were worried of what would happen to their child when one day he would be alone in the world, most did not know what to do about it. A poor lady and mother of a speech-impaired boy had forced her own son to beg. That's what she thought the future for her son would be. That's what she called a way of living for her son. Despite my attempts to counsel her on the importance of education and promising to sponsor the boy's complete schooling, she refused to change her belief.

Parents of a person with a disability need to encourage their child to discover his/ her passion. When it comes to bringing up a differently-abled child, parents need to look at innovative ways of discovering the best for their children. They need to be sensitized on how to handle the emotional needs of their children. More importantly, they need to make conscious efforts to stay positive as parents of a differently-abled child. It is their influence and values which outweigh everything else in the mind of a child.

Suresh Reddy:
Vision of a Future

I cannot see but feel the world;
Please treat me as one among you.
I have my own fears and insecurities;
I have my dreams too.

How many of us get up in the morning and thank God for giving us an opportunity to see the beautiful world? Most of us take our power of sight for granted, don't we? But what happens when a thirteen-year-old boy abruptly loses his eyesight? One day, he is able to see but the very next day, his life is plunged into darkness. Being a son of a farmer with a meagre family income does not help much. Does he sit back and curse his destiny? Or does he defy all odds and dares to dream? Suresh chose the latter. Not only did he survive the greatest setback of his life, he made history by becoming the first ever 100% visually impaired person to get an entry into the elite Indian Institute of Management, Calcutta.

This is a story of his vision for his life – a story of hope, determination and hard work. This is the story of Suresh Reddy.

Suresh Reddy was born and brought up in a small village in Andhra Pradesh. His father was a farmer and the family had

45

Suresh Reddy became a hope for visually-impaired across the nation when he completed his Master's from the prestigious IIM Calcutta. His stint with technology ensured that he crossed all hurdles and met success.

very little income. Things were going fine for them till Suresh accidently fell from the top of a building and within a span of about six months lost his eyesight completely. The young boy suddenly saw his world fall apart. He had to discontinue his studies and cursed his destiny. Those were the darkest hours for his family.

"I was fearful to even move around in my house. I became dependent on my parents for everything. I was dejected and lost faith in life. I brooded over my fate for more than a year. As if that was not enough, suddenly a lot of my loved ones started distancing themselves from me. Life seemed to offer no hope. I kept asking myself 'why me?', 'what now?' but found no answers."

Suresh suddenly saw people's attitude change towards him.

"Society never accepts a visually challenged person. It sympathises with you, de-motivates you, and even advises you to stay at home. Even if we want to move ahead in life despite our limitations, instead of encouraging us, people always try to pull us back. My parents and I were going through testing times and all this sympathy was pulling us back every time we tried to move on."

Even at that stage of his life, Suresh was worried for his family. Even though a lifetime of darkness lay ahead for him, he could not discount the fact that he was the future breadwinner for his family. So no matter what Suresh had gone through, he had to move on not just for his sake, but theirs as well.

"For how long could the family live like that? I could see that the only way I could get back their happiness was to first fight my dejection and be happy myself. I realised that tears would not fill empty stomachs. It was easy to get bogged down by challenges. But if anything, it was only making things tougher for me. I had to find the meaning of this new life. After all my tears had dried up, I decided to get up and give life a second chance. I decided to live again. I told myself that I had lost sight but not hope."

At that time Suresh was oblivious to the challenges ahead. The biggest setback came when he decided to resume his studies. He was refused admission into the mainstream schools. When his parents tried to find a special school for him, they realised that there were only very few Telegu medium schools in Andhra Pradesh which catered to the visually impaired. Suresh thought of moving to Bangalore where there were English medium schools for the visually impaired but his parents were hesitant. How could they let him travel so far all alone, knowing very well that he would not be able to even cross a road by himself? Suresh somehow convinced them that education was very important for his future. They ultimately yielded to his aspirations. Or as Suresh puts it,

"I finally made them believe in my dreams."

Suresh moved to Bangalore and joined a school for visually impaired children where he stayed in a hostel for blind people.

Those were challenging times for him. He needed the support and love of his parents but instead he had to suddenly cope with loneliness and a new environment. He feared if he did not study and get good grades, he would become a liability and things would worsen. Whenever such thoughts tried to overpower him, Suresh would just tell himself:

"Let me think about my bread first and everything else later."

At a later stage of schooling, Suresh wanted to take up the commerce stream but was denied admission citing stringent government guidelines which place restrictions on the disciplines which blind people are allowed to pursue. They are discouraged to study science and commerce. Instead, the education system almost forces them to take up social sciences. Suresh was determined to take up commerce but was denied admission in Bangalore. Luckily, schools in Andhra Pradesh allowed him to do so. It was time for Suresh to shift base again.

But that was not the only challenge Suresh had to face. Till class tenth, Suresh had relied on formal Braille printed textbooks. But there were no such text books for the commerce stream after the tenth class. Also till that stage, the school has the legal responsibility to provide audio books to the visually impaired people. But if they wished to study further, they needed to manage on their own. And how? Perhaps only those who make such policies can tell.

Fortunately, Suresh's friends were very forthcoming. Suresh bought a walkman and a radio to play in class. He gave the same to his friends who would record important portions of the books for him which Suresh would play back and learn. Thanks to his dedication and the earnest support of his friends, he cleared the tenth class in the first attempt itself with sixty percent marks.

In his free time between his class twelfth exam and the beginning of his college term, Suresh did not want to waste time. That is when he learnt to use the computer. Back then in 2000, computers were becoming popular. With the help of the computer reading software 'JAWS', Suresh mastered the use of a computer. It was a big achievement for him as most of his friends were unskilled at using a computer at that time. It was a big kick and motivation for him to be able to do so. In retrospect, it turned out to be one of the best decisions for Suresh, given the importance of computers now.

Among his list of firsts, Suresh has another feather in his cap. He was the first blind person to be given admission to a business course for a Bachelor's degree. Suresh personally met people in the HRD ministry to be able to secure this admission and they encouraged Suresh to study the course. They even offered him a relaxation in grades. Anyone could have happily accepted that relaxation. But Suresh politely declined.

"I told them to give me a chance. I did not need reservation or relaxation."

In college, Suresh had to study with regular students. The transition was tough. While the others easily grasped what the teacher was writing on the board, Suresh struggled. But he never lost hope.

He kept going to the classes. He was confident that if by listening attentively, he could at least get half of what the professors were teaching, he would be able to learn the remaining half on his own, with his friends' help. Initially even the professors were sceptical in having a visually impaired person in their class. His bad grades would after all reflect on their report cards. Suresh had to struggle every minute to prove himself. But he kept telling himself that he had every right to dream and that nothing should get in the way of that.

Fortunately, he made good friends who were ready to help him progress. Each friend in college who was pursuing a Master's degree in some subject made extra efforts to help him. He would often ask them a lot of questions. They felt that teaching Suresh was a wonderful learning experience for them as well.

Like all his previous battles, Suresh won this one too. Not only did he pass out with flying colours, Suresh's success opened gateways for many others like him. The colleges opened up and became more receptive to such students.

All this while, Suresh's parents were his biggest support. Their unconditional love kept him going. Many times when he would feel low, he would think about them and their love. He would request his teachers and friends to tell him motivational stories which helped him persevere.

Getting his first job was not easy either. Most of the companies simply told him they had no policies for employment of a visually impaired person. At a time when companies talk of the principles of equal opportunity and diversity in their pre-placement talks, such responses were a bolt from the blue.

Suresh finally got placed with a company called Catalyst. Initially unsure of his merits and capabilities, they hired him on contract. They told him that only if he did well for one year would they absorb him as a permanent employee. His job was primarily documentation, conducting employee surveys and data management. After a year, Suresh secured the job. Any other person in his place would have been delighted. But Suresh had bigger dreams and he decided not to join the company.

"I liked the work but I was concerned about the company's biases against me throughout the year. I felt as if my disability was being judged every minute. I did not want to work in a place which did not treat me like any other person. I wanted a dignified and respectful existence. It should not feel as if the other person was doing you a favour by giving you a job."

Suresh went on to work with two other companies, one of which was Wipro. There, he was a star performer for most part of his stint. But just when things began to fall into place, Suresh decided it was time to move out of his comfort zone and try something new.

In 2005, Suresh first came to know of the Indian Institute of Management and decided to do go for post-graduation. He immersed himself in preparing for one of the most competitive exams of the county, CAT. And it was no cakewalk.

On the one hand, most of the material would be given as hard copies and Suresh would have to struggle to convert it into an e-format. This meant a huge waste of time, precious time which other students would utilise for their preparations. There would always be a time lag in when he received the books and when he actually could make use of them. Even then, depending on the quality of paper, the optical character recognition software was never hundred percent accurate.

"It was like reading a book which you know was only 80 percent correct."

Suresh would take help of his classmates to understand what the teacher was teaching. Several volunteers came forward to become his scribe. But a lot depended on the communication between him and the scribe. A small misinterpretation on the part of the scribe or a small communication gap could make or break Suresh's future.

To work on questions on data interpretation which were full of graphs and charts was the most difficult. The scribe would try to draw a graph on his hand. Suresh would try to sense the direction of drawing and had to depend heavily on the scribe's understanding of the whole diagram. To add to it was the fact that policy did not allow the scribe to be a friend or a relative and that his academic qualification was to be lower than that of the candidate.

Hurdles were many, but Suresh had only his goal. Suresh believed the ability to succeed was within him.

"I always believe you will truly have your way if you wish to."

With the help of a scribe, Suresh appeared for CAT but could not get a good enough percentile to make it to IIMs, though he would have got admission to other B-schools. But Suresh wanted nothing but the best. There was just one driving force: his extreme optimism.

"If you tell someone you are from an XYZ B-school, people do not pay attention. You are just like any other person in the crowd. But if you tell them you are from an IIM, people look up to you for at least a second if not more. It is for that one second, that one moment of glory that I never gave up. It was not a choice for me. Sleepless nights and lots of

hard work finally paved the way for me. I finally got a good percentile and cracked my interview in IIM Calcutta."

Tremendous optimism and an exemplary attitude took Suresh to his goal.

If you think there are ways, there are ways. If you think there are no ways, you will not find any. Suresh is just a human being and has his own set of frustrations. But those have nothing to do with his impairment. He works twice as hard as anyone else. That's his commitment towards himself.

Till that time, IIM Calcutta did not have proper infrastructure to support a 100% visually impaired student. Over the first few terms, Suresh met teachers from all the departments sensitising them of his need of e-books. The institute adapted soon enough. Right from arranging a scanner for Suresh for converting all his reading material into an online format which Suresh could listen to through JAWS software, to acquiring a tactile adoption kit which helped Suresh visualise graphs, tables, etc – IIM Calcutta was extremely supportive.

On his part, Suresh never made blindness an excuse for missing any exam or assignment. He would listen to presentations, participate in group tasks and deliver class presentations for his evaluations. One week before the exam, he would sit with the person assigned for writing his exam and explain the basic protocol to him.

But in this highly competitive world, Suresh has had his share of tough times. There have been instances when colleagues around him were too busy with their own studies and Suresh had to manage on his own. There were days when he would be left alone in the hostel when the others partied, times when his colleagues undermined his capabilities. While his friends could read, mark important points in the book, reread; Suresh had to listen and grasp things in one go, especially during exams. He could not read only the important points and skim through the rest.

We are well aware what exam pressure does to young students. This becomes even worse in the context of a visually impaired person because of the dependence on scribes. Suresh recalls an incident when one of his exam assistant/scribe did not want to read a case study twice to him. Suresh had a clash with him and the assistant ended up submitting a blank answer sheet. Fortunately, his professor knew him well and could not understand why he had submitted a blank answer sheet. Finally, on hearing things out, he not only reprimanded the assistant but also gave Suresh a second chance.

Suresh got an 'A' in that exam.

In another shocking incident, Suresh was robbed at the Howrah railway station. If being robbed on arrival wasn't enough of an ordeal, Suresh had to ask around for an hour, try and seek help from people just to reach a Government Railway Police booth located fifty metres from the platforms.

"Two men came forward on the pretext of helping me find my way till the prepaid taxi booth. They snatched away my mobile phone and tried to take away my bag. I shouted for help but nobody came forward. I cried and pleaded to a man standing close by. But he said he was busy and walked away. After pleading for an hour for help and not knowing what to do, I frantically moved around and found the nearest railway enquiry booth. I banged on the door for help. A man came out and took me to the nearest railway

police booth. I was told that since the incident had taken
place outside the station building, it did not fall under their
jurisdiction. I would need to lodge a complaint at the nearby
police station. They didn't even heed my request to lend me a
phone to contact someone at the IIM campus."

After almost two hours, Suresh was luckily found by a college junior on the railway station who saved Suresh from further trouble.

The others on the station that day seem more impaired socially than Suresh. They could see, but not Suresh's pain. They could hear, but not his pleas for help Incidents like these put a huge question mark on degrading moral values in Indian society. It seems like the death of our souls, our conscience.

It was on 6 April 2013 that Suresh finally received his graduation certificate from IIM Calcutta. The entire hall gave him a thunderous applause and was filled with respect for this man who had achieved so much. On the stage walked a proud Suresh – an epitome of courage, determination and optimism.

All his fellow students in the blind school had dropped out in school itself. He was the only one to complete a post-graduation and that too from the elite institute, IIM Calcutta.

"I feel great and proud of myself. When a visually impaired
person goes into an academic environment, he is faced with
several challenges. In the long run, an exercise of wallowing
in self-pity does not help a person in academic pursuits.
It does not also change the intensity of hostility in the
environment. On the contrary, it is an attitude problem that
adds to the already existing physical and environmental
constraints."

Technology and the support of his friends have helped him so far. But society at large also needs to welcome a brilliant person like him. Unfortunately, not many seem to be doing that. At a time when corporates talk about their social responsibilities and workforce diversity, many did not even interview him. Even those who shortlisted him rejected his candidature citing their lame policies. Suresh got a job with the Mahindra group, but that was not before multiple corporate institutions refused to even interview him because of his disability.

Why should that be the case, I ask. Hasn't Suresh cleared the same CAT exam as others? Has he not studied the same books? If the college found him competent enough, why are companies being blind to his abilities? Should we be not looking at employing differently-abled people and creating environments where they can flourish?

Today Suresh is at the start of a new journey and is likely to face many more new obstacles on the way. But one thing which will not change is his faith in his abilities. Suresh wants to change the attitude of people towards differently-abled people.

"I request people to treat us at par and give us a chance to be a part of their world. People's sympathy needs to change to a feeling of respect. If I am able to do that somehow, I will rest in peace when I leave the world."

Unfortunately, the most difficult thing to change in this world is people's attitude. Suresh's story reminds me of another person who was denied a job in the agricultural department of Maharashtra government only because he was colour blind; at a time when only five of the thirty-five posts actually needed perfect vision. It was only when he appealed in court that the job was given to him.

More than Suresh's disability, it is the mindset of our society that is beyond acceptance. We know how to sympathise, but not how to help. It's time we look inside. Let not the spirit die; let not Suresh's struggles go in vain.

Suresh can be reached at sureshj2013@email.iimcal.ac.in.

George Abraham:
Nazar ya Nazariya

For what matters to me is not my disability;
But your attitude towards it.
I will not just seek new challenges;
I will live my life to the hilt.

A ten-month-old boy gets affected by meningitis and loses his eyesight. This, however, does not deter him from becoming a proud Stephanian, an ardent cricket fan, a sports freak, the producer of a television serial and the organiser of the first world cup for blind people. A man whose vision goes beyond what you and I can see; George Abraham is a person whose lovely smile reflects his inner satisfaction and peace. George is a man who cannot be bogged down by what he does not have. At the age of 55, when many plan retirement, George is thinking of 'what next' as actively and passionately as a teenager, attending music classes and appearing for vocals exams. For him, the sky is the limit.

I reach George's office to interview him. As I wait to meet him, my attention wanders to the computer room where several people are working on computers with headphones on. I notice that the people have something different about them; they are

George has won many hearts with his smile and is actively making a change in the lives of people through his production 'Nazar ya Nazariya' aired on the national network. His 'Blind Cricket' initiative in India has won many hearts and gotten his name to the Limca Book of Records.

visually impaired. Only later do I get to know that these people are running a helpdesk for the SCORE foundation.

George comes out of his room and extends a handshake. I am intrigued, because although he cannot see me, he extends his hand to exactly where I stand. When I follow him into his room, I notice it is full of trophies, and the walls of the room are covered with photographs of cricket matches. I find George in several of them. I sit and look around before we begin our conversation.

George's parents were working in London when George was born. When George was ten months old, a meningitis infection affected his retina. That it had severely impacted his vision was discovered much later when he started moving around the house and bumping into things. His parents learnt that their child was permanently visually impaired and could see only partially. The worst part was that George's blindness would aggravate with age.

Unlike many parents who would have cursed their destiny, George's parents were extremely positive. They accepted the reality and decided to not let George's blindness become an impediment to their child's success.

They insisted George attend a regular school. His mother read out the texts from school books and his father assisted him with mathematics. They instilled confidence in George and this was to be his greatest strength. They always encouraged him to focus on his talents, his studies, take part in extra-curricular activities and live a normal life. The family finally came back to India when George was two years old. His younger brother was born when George was five.

George's father was a civil engineer and his job required frequent travelling, often to remote areas. His father did not want his frequent transfers to impact George's studies. So the family decided that George stay for a few years in Delhi with his maternal aunt. Later, he moved to Hubli in Karnataka to be with his family.

Talking about the challenges he had to face, George mentions that the biggest challenge was that he could not read properly. But more than talking about the challenges he had to face, he wants to discuss the opportunities he had.

> *"Due to my poor vision, I had to hold the book pretty close to read it. But my friends were helpful. They would share their notes, arrange for group studies and encourage me. I was actively involved in dramatics, sports and music. I was also the fastest sprinter in the 100m race."*

George was passionate about cricket right from his childhood. He could not bat, but bowled extremely well. He was a very fast bowler. He could not see the batsman clearly but could make out a blurred image. Dennis Lillee and Jeff Thomson, two Australian fastest bowlers at that time were his role models. George ate, slept and dreamt cricket. His friends would often joke that any batsman facing his bowling attack would either go back to pavilion or land up injured. George would bowl and another fielder would cover him on the field.

George's face lights up as he recalls his childhood days. A positive environment can sometimes make the impossible possible. Parents' love and the support of teachers and friends can do wonders to one's motivation levels.

George was declared the best all-round student at the time of his passing out from school. He also got admission into St. Stephen's College in Delhi University. This was his second stint in Delhi. He thoroughly enjoyed making new friends and was involved in music, debates and dramatics. As he stayed in the college hostel, he came to have a large circle of friends.

> *"In hindsight, I realised that this circle of friends was and is still one of my key strengths. I still keep in touch with most of them. And I can vouch that there are some very close friends who will stand by me even in my darkest hours. That I believe is my biggest earning in life."*

George's love for mathematics made him pursue his Master's in Operations and Research. Despite being partially blind, he never let his disability be an excuse. He would record books and listen to them; he would put in extra hours to complete his studies.

A big setback for George was the passing away of his mother. George was doing his Master's when his mother succumbed to cancer on the eve of her 43rd birthday. Her demise was the lowest point in George's life. After her demise, his father was left all alone in Kerala. His brother too was not around as he was studying in a different city. George moved to Kerala to be with his father and also started looking out for a suitable job.

That was easier said than done. People were apprehensive and just could not see him as a capable person. People would come home, say flattering things on his face and promise support. But nobody would get back to him. Sometimes the visitors would completely ignore his presence in the room, and offered unsolicited suggestions to his father. Some would suggest his father set up a grocery store for George; others would say that George would be a liability. That was the only time in his life when he actually felt that his visual impairment was coming in his way. People's pity was bringing down his self esteem.

"My dad had lost his life partner and was finding it difficult to come to terms with his loss. Come evening and both of us did not know how to pass time. We would go out for dinner. We would discuss various possibilities for my career. But the best part was that my father never forced me to do anything against my wishes. These testing times brought me closer to my father."

Nine months had passed and with each passing day, George was losing hope and getting restless. And then a miracle happened. One morning, George got up at 4:00 am with a newfound energy within.

"That morning, a voice inside me told that if I really wanted to do something in life, I had to take control of my life rather than relying on others' help. Suddenly, all my doubts vanished."

At 7:30 am, when his father got up, George told him it was time for him to move and take charge of his life. He wanted to go back to Delhi and begin afresh. To his surprise, his father said yes immediately. He asked George to follow his heart. Without asking any questions, without doubting George's ambitions, he simply gave George five hundred rupees and with that, George boarded the next train to Delhi the same day. Perhaps his father realised where his son's happiness lay. If that day he had felt insecure of his son's future and had not let George chase his dream, how different would life have been for George.

A fifty-two hour journey with only five hundred rupees in his pocket and a vague idea of what he wanted to do almost sounds like the making of a Bollywood movie. On his way to

Delhi, George thought hard about what he really wanted to do. George decided to take a shot at the advertising industry. It would give him an opportunity to meet new people and be creative. From the station he headed straight to a cyber cafe where he designed his resume, got it printed and started calling up various advertising agencies.

Delhi provided George the first platform when on day three of his search he managed to meet the head of an advertisement agency. The man liked George's profile and decided to give him a chance.

> *"I was not sure if he had noticed my disability. I asked him whether he had. He said more than my disability, it was my educational background that caught his attention and made him give me a chance. He then asked me how soon could I join. I told him right away. He smiled and asked me to join a week later. I was overjoyed. That day, I celebrated with my friends and brother and we ate out at an expensive place."*

With a meagre starting salary of eight hundred rupees, George started working with ASP (Advertising and Sales Promotion Co.). His job included project management, co-ordination between different teams and planning.

> *"My secretary would read out and type letters for me. I was on a high and never said no to any job I was given. I sincerely believed that if you show people what you can bring to the table, people do not see what you can't. My talent and knowledge, my hard working spirit and my positive attitude did not let people see my disability."*

Alongside, love blossomed in his life too. One of his friends introduced him to Rupa. To their surprise, both realised they knew each other from childhood. They had been family friends and had grown up together. Her family had moved to a different city sometime and they had lost touch.

Sounds like another typical Bollywood love story, doesn't it?

George and Rupa started meeting regularly and before George knew it, Rupa had told her father she wanted to marry George. But convincing her father was not easy. Her father felt she was crazy and stupid to fall in love with a visually impaired person when she could easily find any other 'normal' guy. But when he saw his daughter's firm resolve, he gave in. It was only after she had convinced her parents that she confessed her love to George.

George shares his side of the story,

"It was kind of funny. My father called me up one day and asked me if I knew any girl called Rupa. When I said yes, he told me that Rupa's father had called up with a marriage proposal and asked me if we should accept it. I told him I was coming to Kerala. We would discuss it then."

George met Rupa and discussed the relationship at length with her. The couple got engaged in 1985. In between, George moved to Mumbai to work with some new clients. After spending two years in Mumbai and changing his job, George and Rupa got married in 1986 and settled down in Delhi.

In 1988, came the biggest turning point in George's life.

George and Rupa were expecting their first baby. Rupa was contemplating her life post the birth of the baby. Over the last couple of months, she had felt a strong need to do something

for the blind community. To take this further, George and Rupa
decided to visit a blind school.

> *"The visit to the blind school was the moment of truth in my
> life. It came and hit me like a rock on my head. I realised
> how lucky I was to be born in a family where I had never
> felt handicapped. Everything around me was so positive. My
> parents had given me the best life possible.*
>
> *"But here were these blind children who were dejected,
> rejected by their families and had lost the zeal to live a
> respectful life. I asked some of the teachers about the future
> of those children. The reply was delivered in a monotone,
> 'Few of them make it to university; many of them fall by the
> way side'. Their callous attitude numbed me and I decided
> to do something for these children."*

The couple had walked into the school to see what Rupa
could do for the blind community but walked out with George's
resolve to do something for the kids. Unlike many people, who
leave social service for post retirement, George was eager to
take it up at a young age when he had a lot of energy. He left
his job to take up the cause of visual impairment. He took up
some freelance assignments with various advertising agencies to
support the family.

Rupa also took up a job to supplement the family income. She
told George, "We should do what we really like. I am willing to run
along."

But the difficult part was to actually figure out what they
wanted to do. George started visiting several blind schools across
the country in his quest for knowing more and exploring avenues
for himself. Life had suddenly found a new meaning.

It was on one such visit to the National Institute for Visually Handicapped, Dehradun that George finally found his calling when he got up to the sound of a cricket match.

"Oh my God! I was suddenly in a different world. Cricket! My first love, my calling."

In the madness of his career and life, George had almost forgotten cricket.

"The kids woke up in the morning and played cricket. Went for breakfast, came back and played cricket. Went for classes, came back and played cricket. Had lunch, came back and played cricket. Only bad light made them stop playing. And that too because the umpire could see no more."

When he saw visually-impaired children playing cricket, he instantly knew what he wanted to do. George realised that cricket could be used as an effective tool to develop qualities of leadership, discipline, ambition, confidence, teamwork and competitive spirit, besides contributing to physical fitness, posture and mobility. It would also enable society to see a non-stereotypical image of blind people which is positive and action-oriented. George researched more about the cricket for blind people and came to know that blind cricket was popular at a much localised level.

George throws more light on blind cricket,

"The overall structure of the game remains pretty much the same except there are audio clues designed to help the players. Aids like a rattling ball, underarm bowling, and audio signals given by the umpire and the players turn the

game into a fully audible phenomenon where those who cannot see can act upon the sounds."

George decided he would organise the first national cricket tournament for the blind and formally established the Score Foundation (Society for Communication and Research). Thus began a new journey in George's life. With Rupa's support and love, of course.

Over the next couple of months, invitations were sent to various blind schools to participate in this tournament. George personally met cricketers like Kapil Dev and wrote to Sunil Gavaskar who pledged him their full support. Arranging money was difficult as no one seemed to be interested in cricket for the blind.

He approached many corporate houses but did not get much support. He went to Mumbai to look for sponsorship. Someone gave him the contact number of a lady who worked in Lintas Media Group. George spoke to her over phone. She was short of time as she had to rush for a meeting, she said. George requested her to just hear him out for two minutes, if not more, and it would be enough for him. Their conversation went on for almost two hours. The lady promised her full support and gave him a few leads.

George contacted each one of them, but in vain. As he was leaving Mumbai empty-handed, he called the lady again just to thank her for her support. She asked George if he had found a sponsor. Hearing that he had not, she asked him for half an hour.

Thirty minutes later, George found his title sponsor in Tata Steel. They pledged a sponsorship worth one lakh. George later came to know that the lady herself was the daughter of the Vice Chairman of Tata Steel.

Once the funds came through, the rest was easier. George handled the cricket related work while Rupa handled the hospitality department. One of his close friends, Varghece Chandy did all the administration work.

As many as 350 blind cricketers came to participate in the tournament; each determined to play his best. Though their accommodation was arranged at a not-so-lavish place, no one seemed to care. It was only cricket that was on everyone's mind. Excitement and hope filled their eyes.

Thus in 1990, the first national level cricket tournament for blind people was organised in the country. The man behind all this was George Abraham. The chief guest for the finals was none other than the then leader of opposition, Rajiv Gandhi. Besides Rajiv Gandhi, Russy Mody, Kapil Dev, Arun Lal and many other eminent personalities graced the occasion with their presence. Many people came just out of curiosity to see how blind people could play cricket.

George makes it sound so easy. But all this had taken George a long time, several months of hard work and a determined attitude. George's dream finally came true. The event was registered in the Limca Book of Records.

George did not stop at this extraordinary feat. He went on to serve as the founding chairman of the World Blind Cricket Council (WBCC), set up the Association for Cricket for Blind in India and played a key role in the organisation of the first cricket world cup for the blind in 1998 in India.

He had to go on many foreign trips, hold several rounds of negotiations with ministries, bureaucrats, cricketers, media and several international bodies to convince various countries to organise a cricket world cup for blind people. At that time, there were no set of standards for blind cricket. Each country had its own kind of ball. In some the ball rattled, while in others it made a different sound. It took the board several months to formulate these rules. But George knew it was going to be worth it.

After all these efforts and meticulous planning, the first Kanishka World Cup for the Blind took place in 1998. And this time again, the man behind all this was George Abraham. Each of these achievements is a story in itself.

Through the medium of cricket, George communicated to the world that the real problem was not blindness but people's apathy and attitude. People form myths based on what they hear and read. And there was a need to make people aware of the capabilities of the visually impaired.

The more I was getting to know about his achievements, the stronger was becoming my urge to learn more about this extraordinary man.

Once the blind cricket events became self sustaining, George moved on to his next project – Project Eyeway.

In 2003, George set up an interactive information hub with the objective of providing all the information one might seek about blindness.

"Information is a first step in bringing about a change. Every week, Eyeway receives close to eighty calls at its helpdesk seeking information about blindness. Some of the callers are parents of blind people who want to know how to cope with their child, some are people who have lost their vision and are victims of discrimination by the society. For the latter, if required Eyeway takes up their cases through its legal teams and helps them get justice."

His list of endeavours does not end here. In 2004, Abraham, along with a friend Navroze Dhondy established the Magiktouch

Talent Management Pvt Ltd to identify, groom and promote visually impaired musicians. In 2005, George launched a radio programme called 'Roshni ka Karwan' which was aired on Vivid Bharti. In 2008, it was adjudged the best radio programme in the category "Best Social Responsibility Initiative".

> *"The idea of launching a radio programme was to reach out to more people. The blind people love to listen to the radio. Doing a national programme on the radio gives us a much wider reach."*

Doing all this needs not just the perfect ideas, but also a flawless execution. It is as much about George's leadership as it is about delegation. It is as much his own faith in his team of volunteers as it is about people seeing value in his ideas and joining hands to make them a success.

In 2007, George Abraham was chosen as one of the Limca Book of Records People of the Year for his contribution to the blind community. The latest on his list of achievements is a TV serial called, 'Nazar ya Nazariya' which was aired on Doordarshan in September 2013. The show was anchored by Naseerudin Shah and Harsh Chaya, two prominent actors.

The way the serial came about is nothing short of a miracle. With his background of advertising, George knew the power of television as a medium to reach out to the masses. Long ago, George had written a story called 'Abhilasha' (literally, hope) which he wanted to convert into a television serial. But the same never saw the light of the day because of lack of funding.

Years later in 2011, Facebook connected George to another Stephanian who was working in the film industry. George explained his serial's concept to his friend, who was instantly bought over by the concept. Together, the duo decided they would pitch to get the funding. They approached several corporates but in the age of 'saas-bahu' sagas, no one was willing to put in their money into an honest concept.

But as they say, when you walk in faith, God walks with you.

"I was sitting in my office when I got a call from an old friend. He was calling someone else and had actually dialled my number by mistake. But we got talking. As luck would have it, he had just walked out of a meeting the new Director General of Doordarshan. What was even more miraculous was that this director was an ex-Stephanian and one year junior to me. I quickly arranged a meeting with the director.

"Over a cup of coffee, we revisited our college days. I did not want to bring up the topic of the television programme in the very first meeting. But as I was about to leave, he asked me if I had any idea or if I was interested in doing something in the field of television."

George put forward a formal proposal for the serial and the ball was set rolling.

While I call it a big coincidence, George calls it fate destined to happen. *'Nazar ya Nazariya'* was aired on national television. Watching the serial has altered my outlook towards differently-abled people and helped cast away the darkness in the lives of the visually impaired.

"Through all my efforts, I want to change the outlook of people around the world. We have no control over our disabilities. That is given to us by God. But we do have a

control over what we do with it. Do we sit over it and waste our lives? Or do we go beyond it and live a meaningful life? My parents have given me a life where I never felt handicapped. My mission is to pass on this legacy to millions of other parents. Only then can I be truly happy."

George and Rupa have two beautiful daughters and are spending a happy life. It has been a great learning experience for me to meet this man. I bid him goodbye and come back home with a strange feeling. How often we feel that life has not done justice to us. But here are people like George who smile at life and embrace life in its entirety.

George, I am sure, has already embarked on a new journey in life; the journey of setting newer goals for himself, juggling with new thoughts, ideas and reinventing and rediscovering his potential.

George can be reached at george@eyeway.org.

Disability and Technology

Technology makes life easier for many people, but for differently-abled ones, technology makes life possible. Right from helping them carry on their daily activities easily to providing them a means of mobility, communication, education and even jobs, advancement in technologies and inventions of several gadgets for differently-abled people has the power to create a barrier-free country for this community.

Devices like eye-controlled computers, e-book readers, screen magnifying, reading software, and sticks with sensors are a boon for visually impaired people. Power wheelchairs are a new means of freedom in the lives of wheelchair-bound people. Text-to-speech, text-to-sign language or computer generated voice software and applications provide communication mechanisms for the hearing impaired.

But while we should be proud of such gadgets, the question of affordability, reach and user-friendliness remain. When more than seventy percent of differently-abled people live in rural areas and speak local languages, are they even aware of such advancements? What is the real effectiveness of such gadgets when these do not reach the very people they are designed for? Even if awareness is created, such assistive technologies and devices are not affordable for more than seventy percent of our disabled community. These technologies need to be mass produced to reach economies of scale. Governments need to intervene to distribute such gadgets at a subsidised rate. Adaptation to local languages is another equally critical factor. People need to contribute to make such widespread use of technology possible, by not just financial assistance but also by creating awareness.

In a country known for its IT revolution, technology can play a major role in bridging the gaps between differently-abled and mainstream societies. The sooner this gets implemented, the faster will be the integration of the disabled to contribute to the nation's progress.

Sanjeev Sachdeva:
Let's Make the World Accessible

When life tried to break me down,
I fought back and never quit.
Not just making my own life comfortable,
I have made my Delhi accessibly 'fit'.

I fix up an appointment to meet Sanjeev and reach the Metro station. As I board the metro, so does a woman in a wheelchair. Through elevators, ramps and reserved seats, the Metro makes its services accessible to her. I ask myself, what made me notice this woman today? All these years during my numerous journeys in the Delhi Metro, I would have crossed many such men and women and would not have noticed them. But today I do. That is because today I am going to meet the man who made Delhi a more accessible place. The man who is behind making travel convenient for differently-abled people – Mr. Sanjeev Sachdeva.

Sanjeev, a man in his late forties, is a man of great patience and determination. He picks me up from the metro station and we reach his house. He is escorted by his father. He waits till his helper sets up his wheelchair and lifts him to the chair. Sanjeev cannot move by himself. He wants his face to be cleaned and looks

Sanjeev Sachdeva has worked diligently to make the world more accessible for the differently-abled. His efforts and work in DMRC and other places has won him appreciation at several international forums and also from former Chief Minister of Delhi, Mrs. Sheela Dixit.

at his helper to indicate to him to do so. For a few moments, I am confused. Have I really come to meet the right person? How can this motionless man be behind so many big achievements when he himself needs help for his daily chores? It is difficult to hold back my tears. A person who needs help even to move his hands has done what millions of others are incapable of. Hats off to Sanjeev for all he is. People like him have taught people like me the most valuable lessons in life.

Sanjeev was not born disabled. He was perfectly healthy. He was an average student and had a big circle of friends. He had three brothers who were all well educated and doing well. Life was good for Sanjeev. He was known in his college as a good debater, a singer and one of the best NSS students.

Sanjeev very candidly admits, "*I was not the 'padhaku' types. I did not have much interest in studies.*"

Trekking was his first love. He was a national level trekker and had gone on many difficult trekking expeditions including Leh-Ladakh. It was on one such difficult trek of Amarnath that Sanjeev had a slight difficulty in walking. Someone noticed a limp in his walking. At that time, Sanjeev paid no attention to that observation. But occasionally he would fall while walking. When the frequency of such falls increased, he got medical tests done which diagnosed him with the dreaded rare disease of muscular dystrophy.

"*With my love for trekking, my first reaction to that diagnosis was 'Oh my God, how will I trek now'.*"

At that time, Sanjeev had just taken admission for his Ph.D. and was preparing for the mains of the civil services exams. He went through the inevitable phase of questions – 'why me', 'what next', etc. Strapped and helpless, waves of self pity would wash over him. He was put on heavy medicines and steroids. Sanjeev wrote a very depressing poem 'कल और आज' at that time to vent out his helplessness and depression. Sanjeev still carries the poem in his bag and asks me to pull it out and hold it in front of his eyes. He reads it aloud for me. The words vividly bring out his disappointments at that stage.

खिलता था मैं भी खुशी के आँगन में– वह कल था,
गम ही साथी है अब– यह आज है।
मैं भी चंचल मस्त मगन था– वह कल था,
विकलांग हूँ अब – यह आज है।
रहता था मैं भी कभी किसी के आँगन में– वह कल था,
स्मृतियाँ ही धरोहर है अब– यह आज है।
मैं भी आनंद लेता था पर कृतिका– वह कल था,
खंडर ही शेष है अब– यह आज है।
मुझे भी चाह थी कुछ कर गुजरने की– वह कल था,
हताश, बेबस, लाचार हूँ अब– यह आज है।
फूल था किसी के हृदय का मैं– वह कल था,
धूल हूँ राह की अब– यह आज है।
था सबकी आँखों का तारा मैं– वह कल था,
भोझ हूँ अब दुनियाँ पर– यह आज है।
इच्छा थी मुझे जीने की– वह कल था,
...– यह आज है।

"Considering my love for travel, my grandfather used to call me the 'foreign minister' of the family. Suddenly, I was stuck at home and had become the 'home minister'."

Sanjeev smiles but I can sense the pain behind it. I cannot reciprocate his smile. I can only feel the depth of his emotions and fall silent.

For Sanjeev, the going was tough. Society made his life even more difficult. He would hate it when people would come home and sympathise with him and his family. Many told him to start reading religious books. At the age of 23, he was expected to give up on life and become a saint. Slowly, his friends started abandoning him too.

"Whenever I would go out, people would look at me; some with sympathy and others with curiosity. Some would even mock. I could tolerate neither and would abuse them. I could not see myself as a source of entertainment and pity for the society."

Life continued on a slow and tragic pace and left Sanjeev lonely. Darkness engulfed him. Everything seemed meaningless. But for how long could he go on in this state of mind? Did he want to live his entire life as a patient? Sanjeev asked himself this question and tried to find a solution within him. After months of soul searching and introspection, he decided to go out and meet people. Destiny brought him closer to Mr Rajinder Johar (whose story is also covered in the book). When he saw a man who was bed-ridden for life running an NGO for disabled people, he asked himself why he was cribbing. Sanjeev felt he was so much better than Mr Johar and yet, unlike Mr Johar, all he was doing was complaining, abusing and brooding over his destiny. He started working with Mr. Rajinder. Through him he met many more disabled people. Slowly he began to pull out of his own issues to look at the larger world.

But if there was anything which could pull Sanjeev out completely, it was his love and passion for travel. He formed a group of travel enthusiasts and planned a holiday. Only that this time, all the co-travellers were disabled people.

"I remember the first trip I did post the traumatic happening. My mother had gone to meet a relative after ten years. It made me realise how my disability had not just affected me deeply, but my family too. I decided to travel more frequently not just to give myself a breather, but also to give my family one, especially my mother. Travel worked as the best therapy for me. Any long weekend I got, I would make advance plans to travel."

Travel also made him realise that Indian tourism was out of bounds for disabled people. At home, one could get every small thing adjusted according to one's needs. But travel was like an Agni Pariksha. As his travel frequency increased, so did his sensitivity to all these issues. That perhaps was the turning point in Sanjeev's life. He decided to do something about it.

His became the voice of the disabled traveller community. He started raising his concern on such issues and became an activist. Instead of only presenting problems, Sanjeev suggested solutions to make the country disabled-friendly.

"Like a hungry child who craves for food, I crave to make my country more accessible. I am a firm believer in the Indian government institution. I do not believe in criticising them, but in collaborating with them.

"I feel accessibility has not just a social but also an economic dimension. It is not just the disabled people but all the people vulnerable to restrictions - the elderly or pregnant women or those recuperating from an ailment. Such people together make up a significant percentage of the population. Surely, anybody marketing an idea would like to keep these potential customers in mind, be it in theatres or shopping

complexes or resorts. I believe businesses will appreciate the sound economic sense in making their establishments accessible to all."

Sanjeev's thought process and work have got him noticed and brought him various interesting opportunities. In 2000, he was invited by the United Nations Economic and Social Commission for Asia and the Pacific, UNESCAP to present a paper on accessibilities in Bali. The Bali Conference adopted the Bali Declaration which placed the issue of barrier-free environment for persons with disabilities on the agenda of the UNESCAP countries. This was followed by training on accessibility in Bangkok. All these experiences further prepared him to do something back in his own motherland.

To begin with, Sanjeev started working with Delhi Tourism to make Dilli Haat the first disabled-friendly tourist spot of India. Thanks to his efforts, the Archaeological Survey of India made it mandatory to ensure disabled-friendly access at all sites and monuments maintained by it. After this, there was no stopping Sanjeev. He worked with the government at various levels to make the entire country disabled-friendly. Some projects failed, some succeeded. But Sanjeev kept going.

Since then, Sanjeev has presented various papers on accessibility in other countries like Indonesia, Japan, Sri Lanka, Hong Kong and Canada. He has worked with various institutions including the IITs. He has done a lot of research and published papers on the Indian Railways, road safety, buses and bus shelters. Whenever, an unfortunate disaster takes place in the country, Sanjeev tries to travel to such areas to train and sensitise people to take care of those who get disabled in the calamity.

When the planning for Delhi Metro began, Sanjeev and his colleague Anjlee Agarwal were made a part of its planning and feasibility study right from the initial stages. They shared practical recommendations with the DMRC (Delhi Metro Rail Corporation) on making travel accessible for the disabled of the city and did several accessibility audits during the planning and trials of the Delhi Metro. As a result of their efforts and constant engagement with DMRC, the Delhi Metro is disabled-friendly today.

In 2002, Sanjeev received the National Award as the best employee in the category of the orthopedically disabled by none other than the former President of India, Dr APJ Abdul Kalam. He has also received the Red and White Bravery Gold Award in 2005, and CevinKare Ability Mastery Award 2005 amongst others.

"I am happy and content with my life. I no longer abuse people when they see me. In fact, I smile at them."

On the personal front, Sanjeev is single. His mother left for her heavenly abode a couple of years ago. And that has been the biggest setback in Sanjeev's life.

"Mothers are always special. My mother devoted her life to my care. I would wake her up many times during the night – sometimes asking for water and sometimes asking her to help me change sides. She would do so without any anger or irritation. I distinctly remember a night when I asked my mother to help me change sides. She said she did not want to get up as her chest hurt. But I insisted. Finally, she got up and helped me. But soon her pain became

unbearable. She was taken to the hospital where we got to know that she had just suffered a heart attack. Such is the love of a mother. No matter how old you become, there is one lap to which you can always go back and lie down on like a child."

Sanjeev's mother left him six years ago and 2008 was the toughest and the loneliest year of his life. The most important person in his life had passed away. Even at the age of forty-eight, he remembers his mother as fondly as a four year old child.

Sanjeev now stays with his father and attendants. His brothers visit whenever they can. He wonders how he would cope without his father. Parents are the biggest support for all of us but more so for people with disabilities. Because even when the world leaves us alone to cry, parents wait for our smiles to return.

While at home, he does not meet anyone or take calls post 8 pm. He loves to be alone and at peace with himself. He is a great fan of SAB TV and likes to end his day with laughter by watching comedy serials.

Sanjeev earns decently enough but is not able to save much of it. Whatever he earns is spent on his attendants and drivers. He has many medical requirements, including the need for physiotherapy sessions which cost a lot. He is also a diabetic now. Despite that, he loves his rajma chawal and peanuts.

"Life is not the same with age catching up. I have become more mature. I have increased my scope of work from accessibility to holistic disability management. I am proud to be a tax payer of the country. I look forward to a society where all disabled people are employed and become tax payers of the country."

Sanjeev calls his powered wheelchair, 'Freedom'. With it, he is on his own without any attendants to eavesdrop.

Sanjeev smiles and adds, *"Especially when I am on a date."*

Sanjeev's candid confessions lighten the mood in the room.

"I have more plans to do things. I will raise awareness on the issue of disability. Life is too short. The government is doing its bit. The media has played an important role. A beginning has been made. Movies now show disabled people not just as villains but heroes. Black, Guzaarish, Barfi – have made a positive difference."

Sanjeev Sachdeva has achieved so much in his life for millions of people around him. He has touched many lives.

"I take life as it comes. Every day is a new beginning. My tagline: ' स्वस्थ रहो, वयस्त रहो, मस्त रहो*' (Be healthy, busy and happy)."*

Words fall short when Sanjeev finishes his story. My tears are not tears of pity, but of pride. I am happy to be a miniscule part of Sanjeev's journey. People like him smile and make you wonder,

"A lifetime is a long enough period to do something meaningful. Why should I spend it cribbing when I can spend it smiling? Live life king size. It comes only once."

Sanjeev can be contacted at sanjeevsach@hotmail.com.

Neeru Gautam:
Disability with Dignity

I need your love and attention;
I crave for a respectful living.
That's what has been conferred to me;
That's what to the society I am giving.

From the glamour of the fashion industry to the four walls of a room, the transition was not smooth for Neeru Gautam. At an age when a girl dreams of a great career and a loving husband, Neeru suddenly found herself confined to her bed. The four walls of her room and a mobile phone became her life. After depriving herself for twelve long years, Neeru decided to live again. So what if she could not stand on her feet? What if the world had labelled her as 'disabled'? Her wheelchair would be her best friend. Neeru got through the tough times, thanks to the care and love of her family and friends. So she decided she would provide the most valuable gift of a care-giver, ('*sahyogi*', as they are known) to others like her. She began counselling, and tried bringing love and care to the lives of many others like her. She wanted to make sure they did not live life with difficulty, but with dignity. Her story is as much about happiness as it is about pain; as much about hope as it is about frustrations; as much about smiles as it is about tears.

❖

While Neeru's smile enchants everyone around her, she has made her power chair her best companion. she trains caregivers to enable a dignified living for the differently-abled.

Neeru was adored by everyone in the family, and was a spoilt kid. She was on the way to becoming a designer and was planning to open her own boutique in Delhi. She had also just been offered the franchise of a popular fitness centre. With everything falling into place just as she had wanted, Neeru was on cloud nine.

When a mild fever gripped her, she did not think too much of it. But when the same lingered for more than three months, Neeru's parents were worried. No medicine seemed to be working. Her condition worsened when the fever translated into sudden memory loss and hypersensitivity. The doctors were clueless about her condition and could not gauge what was wrong. The tests did not seem to yield any results. Neeru then developed bladder complications and was hospitalised for over a month.

Neeru's brother was about to get married. But the family decided to postpone the wedding till Neeru recovered. Little did they know at that time that their daughter was gradually becoming paralysed. Finally, an MRI of her spinal cord revealed a swelling in her spine. She was given medicines for tuberculosis. Her condition began to improve but when the medicines were stopped, the symptoms reappeared.

> *"My fate was sealed when the doctors announced their verdict. I had a progressive and incurable disease – an advanced form of tuberculosis. I could not be treated. I did not care about the medical terminologies or jargon the doctor coldly used to convey the problem. All I knew was that he was asking me to accept my fate; telling me my life was over."*

With the passage of time, Neeru could no longer even walk. Was it a bad dream, or some cruel joke? How could it happen all of a sudden? How could the doctors just pronounce the verdict with so much apathy? Surely, there could be a way out; some medicine, some surgery.

> *"I had planned to become a designer, get married and start a family. Being disabled was not part of the plan. And yet, there I was; lying still and helpless; seeing all my plans crushed before my eyes. Why?"*

Neeru had no answers.

> *"I still remember the day my parents took me to a hospital where some of the patients were admitted for similar disabilities. The sight there was frightening. For a moment, I prayed to God that if this was going to be my fate, He should just take me away."*

For the doctors in the hospital, it was business as usual. They told her parents that Neeru's problem was incurable. She was still better of the lot, but her condition would only worsen. The words of a doctor can make or break a patient's will power. Neeru's doctors gave her no hope and their sharp words affected not just the young lady's confidence, but also dashed the hopes of her parents.

For anybody who could walk till a few months ago, suddenly being confined to a wheelchair could be the most dreadful thing in life. So it was for her. Life changed thereon. Her parents became especially protective of her. The lack of awareness on dealing with this condition confined Neeru to the four walls of the house.

From driving and travelling extensively, she started painting and knitting. Days became longer, nights scarier. The television remote and her phone became her world. At times, she would call up telephone operators just to know if it was day or night outside the room. When she would hear the drops of rain outside, she would call the operator to confirm whether it was raining.

Often the world sees a differently-abled person in isolation. But it affects his or her entire family. At home, her parents were going through an equally difficult phase. When someone would suggest the name of a doctor, temple or priest, they would simply rush to seek consultation and blessings for their daughter. When someone recommended changing the layout of the home to be Vaastu-compliant, they went to the extent of rebuilding their house from scratch.

> *"I got a lot of support from my family and friends. On the days I had to go to the hospital, I would feel elated. I used to think of it as an outing and wear my best clothes to the hospital."*

The period from 1996 to 2008 was the loneliest period of her life. After twelve long years of fighting her disability, Neeru finally decided to give life a sincere chance. Her hospital connected her to NGOs working for the cause of disability. She was introduced to the Sahyogi scheme, whose mission was to provide care to care-seekers. Soon, she started thinking of doing something beyond her own survival.

> *"A disabled person cannot depend on his/her parents for every small need. It bogs him down and negatively impacts his life. For a disabled person to live a dignified life, things need to be handled much more professionally. Caregivers need special training to cater to the physical and mental needs of their ward."*

In India, there is a huge mismatch between the number of disabled people looking for someone to care for them to the actual number of professional care-providers. According to a study done by WHO, India is among the 57 countries worst hit by shortage of trained caregivers. Neeru's efforts thus brought a ray of hope in the lives of many.

Coming from her own experiences, the entire concept of Sahyogi instantly appealed to her. The objective was to build a support system for differently-abled people. She also realised that counselling was a crucial aspect not just for the differently-abled person, but his/her family as well. Neeru started counselling people when they were in hospitals and had just been diagnosed so that they walked out more aware and better prepared. The more she trained the care givers, the more she felt fulfilled. She started forgetting about her own issues, engaging with others like her.

Speaking about Sahyogi, Neeru tells about the different challenges they faced.

> "From small things like the caregiver being strong enough physically to lift the ward for his or her bowel and sanitary needs to the person sharing the same meal preference as the ward (as they might double up as the cook), each little detail matters.
>
> "In fact, it is so difficult to find all these things in one person that most people end up keeping more than one caregiver. For example, they employ one to take care of their sanitary needs and another computer literate person who can answer their emails.
>
> "Another problem arises when the bond between the caregiver and the care-seeker grows to an extent that the latter becomes emotionally dependent on the former. If

the care-seeker needs to take even a day off, life comes to a standstill for their ward. So much so that when the caregiver decides to leave, it's a huge setback for the disabled people. Sometimes the caregiver even tries to exploit this situation.

"My own caregiver had only studied up to the eighth standard when he came to me. I got him admitted to a computer course, an English course and tried to help him progress in life. But when the guy became skilled, he left saying that now he could find better jobs. For Sahyogi, training these caregivers is as much about inculcating a feeling of love, care and compassion towards their masters."

Neeru is now working towards an on-service training module for the caregivers for a faster and more fruitful deployment. In a country where disabled people struggle to lead a dignified life and where there is a scarcity of trained professionals to attend to people with special needs, Neeru's work helps people live a joyful life.

Neeru's disability had made her leave college mid-way. Inaccessibility of the transport system and college buildings had confined her to her home. Right from designing wheelchair friendly university buses to organising sensitization workshops for the transport department, and also participating in audits of important places and buildings of the city, Neeru is doing all it takes to ensure that no other Neeru stays home.

But Neeru's personal life throws open a plethora of questions for society. Neeru says she is happy staying single and enjoying life with her friends. But there is more to this statement than her choice of staying single.

"See Disha, let me be honest. If I ask you to choose between two friends when you decide to go shopping – one who is

healthy and the other who is disabled and will need your help to get on the car, get down at the market, whose wheelchair you will have to steer, who cannot eat the same food as you do as his or her body cannot digest a lot of stuff – whom would you choose?

"Marriage is also like that. An abled person may not be able to spend a lifetime with someone who is wheelchair-bound. And if I have to marry a differently-abled person, why can't I simply stay single and enjoy life like that with this person. He would be my best friend. What will we achieve by getting married?"

Even though I do not completely agree with what Neeru feels, I do not question her further. Neeru's questions leave me speechless and numb. We as a society are not ready to take on the responsibility of a differently-abled friend, leave aside making them our life partners.

My sadness is short lived as Neeru shows me photographs with many of her friends. Truly the smiles on their faces and the joy in their eyes are worth sharing.

I am overwhelmed to learn about Neeru's journey from a once-bubbly girl-next-door to a lonely girl who was cheated by her destiny, and finally to being a true friend to many. We end the interview as Neeru has plans to spend the evening at India Gate enjoying her freedom with her Wheelchair Flying Club friends who roam about Delhi on their power wheelchairs and tell the world,

"We are one of you. Only our mode of movement is different…"

Neeru can be contacted at neeru.sanjeevani@gmail.com.

Disability and Accessibility

A simple knee injury which restricts one's movements for a day is difficult to bear for a person. A hearing problem which stops a person from communicating with his family for a day can be frustrating. A person's sore throat which prevents him from speaking can spoil his day. It is an almost impossible task for a pregnant woman to climb four floors to reach her office. A disabled person faces these situations day in and day out. The only difference in this case is that he cannot stay home. He has to face these obstacles as he needs to go out and earn his living. He needs to communicate with others not just for personal, but professional reasons as well. He needs to work as any other person does for a decent living.

In a country like ours, with almost 55 million people facing these issues on a day-to-day basis, a country whose disabled people outnumber the entire population of France, why is it that 95 percent of our buildings are still constructed without due diligence to the concept of accessibility? It is interesting to note that making a building disabled friendly adds only 2 percent to the total cost of the building. Why is it that ramps, railings, Braille prints, slip resistant floorings, audio visual signs and so on are not taken into account when building schools, colleges, offices, tourist places, shopping complexes, restaurants, bus stands and even hospitals? Shouldn't every bank and hospital have a sign language interpreter? How is a differently-abled person supposed to explain his illness to a doctor in the absence of such basic services?

Their voices are often ignored by people sitting in important customer-facing roles. Many cannot go to schools without assistance. It is no wonder then, that when a differently-abled child is born in a house, all that the parents think of is the survival of their child. No wonder such children are protected and not allowed to step out of their homes to live their dreams.

All the people in this book have shown how accessibility can have an impact on their lives. A little cooperation by the school, college authorities, and corporate houses helped them fulfil their dreams and go beyond the ordinary. It not just makes social but also economic sense for India to grow and prosper. For how else do we claim to be a world-class economic power?

If this country truly has to take inclusive growth seriously, it is time we pay attention to these 55 million. It is time we make our country barrier-free for all our country men.

Sukhsohit Singh:
Fight for what is truly yours

The world may try to cage me;
I fly, I dream, I set myself free.
To every lock called 'obstacle';
I find a key named 'opportunity'.

When the world writes you off, the urge to prove yourself lights a fire. When people say you can't walk, there is an urge to fly.

He may have cracked one of the toughest exams of the country but the government did not deem him 'fit' enough. The civil services selection committee rejected his application not on merit, but on medical grounds. But Sukhsohit stood up to fight for what was truly his. His persistent fight not only rocked the government but also struck chords with millions across the globe. Somewhere Sukhsohit knew that he had to bring about a revolution and wanted to win not just for himself but for the entire community of the differently-abled. And it was this desire to bring a positive change that kept him going. Today Sukhsohit has become the first genetically disabled person to be part of the Indian Civil Services. Sukhsohit's fight against the whole bureaucratic system brings out the short sightedness of our policies and policy makers, especially when it comes to genetic

Sukhsohit beat Thalassemia and went on to become the first genetically disabled person in the Indian Civil Services. He fought for his rightful place and ensures that merit of others is aptly acknowledged too.

disabilities. His victory is a symbolic message that no matter how difficult the road is and howsoever less travelled, if one really wants to achieve something, there is no obstacle that cannot be conquered.

Sukhsohit was born in Chandigarh. His father was an Air Force officer. Sukhsohit was the younger son in the family. At the time of his birth, the doctors did not diagnose anything unusual or wrong with the baby. But with the passage of time, the little boy companied of breathless and tiredness. He was diagnosed with Thalassemia Major.

Thalassemia is a genetic disorder in which one's body does not produce red blood cells. Those inflicted with this disorder have to undergo regular blood transfusions throughout their lives and are susceptible to a large number of infections owing to low immunity levels. It is one of the major killer diseases across the world. Even people who survive have a hard life ahead of them. Unfortunately, there is hardly a reliable, affordable treatment for this disease.

It was a big bolt for Sukhsohit's parents. His father had seen several hardships in his life. His father had been orphaned at the age of four, his grandfather had been killed during the Partition. His grandmother too had been attacked then and her shoulder was completely damaged. And now he saw his dearest child suffer. He did not know how long Sukhsohit would survive. Even if he did, what kind of a life would he have to lead? For any parent, it is traumatic to see his or her child suffer. At a stage when most parents buy new clothes for their children, Sukhsohit's parents bought medicines and syringes. At a stage when most parents take their child to play, Sukhsohit's parents would take him to hospitals.

But despite the difficult circumstances, his father kept telling himself that nothing can be debilitating unless you yourself allow it to be.

Sukhsohit spent the initial few years of his life in the Air Force School, Delhi. Owing to his own upbringing, he never felt inferior to other children. His parents had made his teachers aware of his condition so his teachers expected him to be a quiet and dull child. But he would want to play like other children. He participated in various competitions in school and was a bright student right from his childhood.

Bringing up a Thalassemic child is not easy for the parents. The lifelong trips to the hospital, regular blood transfusions, daily medicines and several other complications make it not just a financial burden, but also an emotionally disturbing experience for the entire family. The family visited several hospitals in search of a cure. Unfortunately, there is only one reliable cure for this disease, – one's sibling's bone marrow can be transplanted into one's body. Not only is it extremely difficult to find an exact match with the sibling's bone marrow, but also it cost almost 18 to 20 lakhs to undergo the bone marrow transplant. It was unthinkable amount at that time, given Sukhsohit's family's humble background.

"My parents would save each rupee with the hope that someday they would be able to get a bone marrow transplant done and see me hail and hearty. Right from which soap we would buy to whether we would eat out, every small decision was influenced by these cost-saving considerations. However, despite all efforts, my brother's bone marrow did not match mine and that was the end of all our hopes."

There was lack of awareness of this disease and hardly any known paradigm of treatment in the medical fraternity at military hospitals at that time. Eventually, his father got in touch with an NGO in the Post Graduate Institute of Medical Research (PGIMR) in Chandigarh. The Thalassemia Children Welfare Association was a well-known NGO for people afflicted with this genetic disorder. Sukhsohit's father got himself transferred to Chandigarh so Sukhsohit could be brought up under the care of expert doctors.

This came with its own sets of compromises and troubles for the family. Their house was quite far off from the main city and Sukhsohit's elder brother had to travel close to two hours a day to reach school. Sukhsohit could not afford to overexert. So he was admitted in a nearby Kendriya Vidyalaya. It was here that he completed his education. Even though he had to miss school often for his treatment, he was always among the top performers in the school. What he could not achieve in sports, he compensated through academic excellence. Even though Sukhsohit's school was a Hindi medium one, the desire to learn and excel in English made him put in a lot of hard work. Books became his best friends.

While in college, Sukhsohit did not want to be given any special treatment by his college or friends. He never disclosed his ailment to his friends at college.

> "I believe the world is a great buyer of your happiness but not your problems. I never wanted to share my problems with anyone. I didn't want any sympathy or pity. Thus, I did not even tell my closest friends about my problems. Often, I would go in the evening to give my blood sample and the next evening to collect the blood and get the transfusion done."

He aptly summarises his thought process through the following lines,

"अपने ज़ख्मों की यूँ नुमाइश न कर,
जो चाहता है, उसे पाने की फरमाइश न कर,
जो तेरा है ख़ुद चल कर आएगा तेरे दर पे,
उसे पाने की पल पल यूँ गुज़ारिश न कर।"
(Do not disclose your wounds to others, do not disclose your hopes and wishes either. Whatever is deservingly yours will be yours.)

His deep thoughts speak volumes about the peace Sukhsohit feels within, the balance and the wonderful temperament. For it becomes difficult to lead a normal life when your body feels weak, when the slightest injury can take months to heal and when medicines are as integral part of the diet as your meals.

"Pain is inevitable, suffering is optional. I feel that many a time even if a person with a disability wants to live a normal life, his family loses hope and tries to pull him or her out of the system. In my case, I told my parents to let me live life on my own terms. My mother was always over concerned about my health. But I requested her that I would prefer to live a short but independent life than a longer life being dependent on them. It took me many patient conversations with her to make her feel confident of letting me be on my own, though each time some relative or neighbour would come and try to shake that confidence. But I never wanted to compromise on the quality of my life just because others were sceptical."

Unlike most Thalassemia patients who drop out of school at an early age, Sukhsohit completed his honours in Business Economics and also secured the first rank in the Income Tax examination. He also got first position when he completed his Masters in Public Administration and qualified for the UGC's Junior Research Fellowship.

Sukhsohit wanted a platform from where he could make a difference not just for himself or his family but for the entire country. So he started preparing for civil services. He first appeared for the exam in the year 2007 but could not clear it. He reappeared in 2008 and got a good rank. However, the results were delayed by a few months. By then Sukhsohit had joined as a Junior Research Fellow in Punjab University. He reapplied in 2010. When the results came out in September 2010, his name was in the list of successful candidates.

When a person sees his name on that elite list, it is like a dream come true. But when Sukhsohit saw his name, he smiled to himself and prepared to get ready for the tougher part. Till date, no one with a history of Thalassemia had been able to clear the civil services interview. This was going to be an epic case for the selection committee to deal with.

While Sukhsohit knew he could not get into some of the on-ground profiles like those of the Indian Police Services, he also felt that there should be no reason why he could not even be considered for non-technical roles. Sukhsohit's fears came true when the medical board rejected his application citing his disability. Sukhsohit believed he deserved better treatment.

When any other person in his place might have given up, Sukhsohit decided to fight the system. He filed a petition with the Education Ministry seeking reconsideration of his case. Nothing happened and his petition fell on deaf ears. It was lost in the heaps of files. That was until Sukhsohit decided to take the help of the media.

The media helped him greatly in his cause. His story was covered by prominent newspapers. When his case came out in the media, the entire nation joined him in his struggle for his rights. Soon, a lot of his supporters were on the streets, petitioning and demanding the logic behind his disqualification.

On World Blood Donation Day, Sukhsohit was called to the Apollo Hospital to welcome the Chief Guest who happened to be the Minister of Health in the Delhi government. It was then that Sukhsohit spoke to him with frankness and firmness.

He told the minister how it was not his rejection which perturbed him but the reasons given for his rejection. The first reason given was that his life span could not be predicted and he might have a short life. In the event of his withdrawal from duties or death, the concerned department would be in a chaotic situation. Sukhsohit politely asked the minister if the minister or the person giving this reason was sure of his own life, health and survival. With life by definition being unpredictable, this reason was ridiculous. The minister fell silent. Sukhsohit tried to allay the minister's fears by explaining that with proper medicines and lifestyle, Sukhsohit was leading a normal life.

The second reason given for his rejection was that his treatment cost would be a liability to the government. Here again, Sukhsohit had a fair point. He jokingly said that as his father was a senior officer in Air Force, so even if he did not make it to the civil services, he was still likely to continue as a liability to the government.

"I then laughed and told them that they may as well extract something out of me instead of just paying for my medical expenses."

Sukhsohit's witty replies got the minister's attention and he promised Sukhsohit help in all possible ways. But nothing much came out of it.

Despite all these odds, Sukhsohit persisted. Media's constant support and Sukhsohit's patience and determination finally culminated in the Prime Minister personally intervening in the case.

On 1 July 2011, Sukhsohit finally got a selection letter from the Indian Defence Accounts Services. An impossible feat had just been made a reality by the never say die spirit of this young man. A man *we* call disabled.

Thanks to his background and the interesting journey of getting into the services, everyone in the Army had already heard of him and he was much respected. Everyone knew he was a man of strong will and could not be taken lightly.

Since his induction, Sukhsohit has been travelling all across the country for his training. How does he manage his transfusions during his constant travel?

Wherever he has to stay at a place for more than twenty days, he plans the transfusions in advance. He tries to arrange contacts in the hospitals. The department has also been very forthcoming and makes the necessary arrangements. A little advance planning and care, proper medication and a healthy lifestyle helps Sukhsohit lead a good life.

I ask if this is a mission fulfilled for Sukhsohit?

Sukhsohit smiles,

"There was a time when my parents were worried for me. They used to tell me they would start a computer centre or a 'kiryana' shop for me so I could earn a livelihood even when they were gone. 'Career' was a privilege reserved only for my elder brother.

"And now, when I go home in a car with a red beacon, my parents' eyes are filled with pride. So personally I am satisfied. Often, we curse God, but I firmly believe that if he takes away one thing he is willing to give it back to us in a hundred other ways. We also need to work towards our dreams, passionately and with determination."

Sukhsohit's victory is only a milestone and the journey has just begun. Medical apartheid in India is a grave problem. India's disability bill does not even consider genetically disabled people under the special quota for disabled people. There is a reservation quota for the locomotive, hearing, speech and visually handicapped. But nothing for people who are not by definition physically handicapped. Sukhsohit is now an activist, fighting for the rights of genetically disabled people. He is lobbying with authorities to get the Disability Bill passed in Parliament and creating awareness among people by writing in magazines and journals. Sukhsohit brings forth an interesting observation when he says,

"When two people who are Thalassemia minors marry; one in every three child born is a Thalassemia minor. So, if some basic tests are done upfront, we would have this disease totally wiped out."

In a country where people prefer to get a *kundli* match before marriage, it is not surprising that there is no concept of a medical match. We need to create awareness about these facts among people. The government needs to play an active role in that. The blood screening test before the conception of a child should be made mandatory and affordable. People need to be sensitised about the significance of blood donations. Like polio, Thalassemia can be completely eradicated.

Sukhsohit adds further that there have been instances when Thalassemia patients have been administered blood infected with AIDS.

In a country beginning to establish its reputation as a global brand for medical infrastructure, such neglect and absence of strict medical laws is unacceptable. India houses close to thirty million Thalassemia patients and accounts for ten percent of the world's diseases. Are we as a society blind to people who are less privileged? Why can't we make lives simpler for differently-abled people? Simple steps like having classrooms for these people on the ground floor, installing elevators and keeping their doctors' and parents' contact numbers handy are small steps which can prevent many students from withdrawing from schools at an early stage.

Sukhsohit is very optimistic that things can change, provided there is more awareness. He has embarked upon an important road – the road to make lives easier for millions others like him; the road to create many more Sukhsohits who do not need to fight the system to achieve what they truly deserve.

As Sukhsohit optimistically puts it,

"All of us have a spark within, waiting to be ignited. Our endeavour should be to turn that spark into fire and give wings to that fire. To fly high and touch the sky. The winning

horse doesn't know why it runs. It runs because of the lashes and beating – the pain given to it by its jockey. God is the jockey who guides and rides us. So whenever you are in pain, just believe that God wants you to win the race."

Sukhsohit can be contacted at sukhsohit_2020@yahoo.co.in.

Disability and Indian Policies

While researching the topic of disability, I read about the policies for the disabled and how our Indian laws look at disability. While most policies do make an honest attempt in making India a more inclusive society, many glaring questions still remain.

The first and foremost is the basic issue of counting. Do you know that different independent surveys place the percentage of disabled people in the country at vastly different numbers? Some state the numbers to be around twenty million while some state them to be as high as seventy million. Again, there is a lot of discrepancy as to which disabilities are counted under these surveys. Some people may be hundred percent impaired, while others might be partially impaired. Some disabilities may be obvious, while the genetic or psychic are not. I also found out to my shock that there are no words in Telegu or even Hindi for mentally-disabled people. How is the calculation done in such states and areas where people understand only local languages? Many policies are thus based on numbers which may or may not be accurate.

Another point of concern is the exclusion of genetic disability altogether in the Persons with Disability Act, 1995. Sukhsohit could not claim his legal rights simply because legally he was not counted in the 'disabled' category and technically he was not counted as a non-disabled person. How do we deal with such glaring discrepancies? And why has it taken us so long to do something about it? Why do such basic policy gaps exist?

Even in areas where policies exist, they are mere legal acts without being properly implemented; policies for which governments have never been held accountable and policies which have not been discussed and debated in the Parliament. Ministries exist for social justice and disabled community. But they are often sidelined in day-to-day government functions, simply because they are not considered important enough.

Is it because disabled people do not form a significant part of our vote bank? Why is there no policy to make it easier for a disabled person to go out and cast his vote? Why is there no policy to make it a responsibility of the government to help these people become an active part of our electoral process?

Such questions, and many more, still remain unanswered.

K. Murali:
Sound of Silence

Beyond the world of words and sounds;
Hear the sound of silence.
Listen too to the music in my life;
For here you will find love in abundance.

Happiness brings a song to our lips. When we are sad, we talk to someone close to us and express our pain through words. Words connect; words bind. After food, water and shelter, communication is perhaps the next most basic need of a human being.

Thus, when I first heard about Mr. Kuppusamy Murali, my first instinct was that here was a man who could have gone into oblivion because he cannot hear people speak, nor can he express himself through words. He could be the most unnoticed person in his circle. How he managed to achieve so much in life is nothing short of a miracle. Championing the cause of sign language at the national level is not an easy job, nor is caring for the education, employment, matrimony of thousands of hearing-impaired men and women. Through the extraordinary institute called Deaf Leaders, Murali has managed to help several others like him to live their dreams. Not only are his achievements exemplary, they also speak volumes about the pillar of humanity that Murali is.

K. Murali has worked to make the world more sensitive to signs and symbols, for those who cannot hear or speak. He continues to bring smiles and create opportunities for hearing and speech-impaired through 'Deaf Leaders'.

Interviewing Murali was one of the most challenging experiences of my life. It was the first time I had to understand someone's emotions without him uttering a word. I had to appreciate the unspoken. I had to communicate with him without saying or hearing anything. Something I had never done before. What complicated things further was that we were meeting for the first time.

This difficult task was also a valuable lesson for me. By not understanding sign language, I was cut off from millions across the globe. I wondered if work would wait till such a person arranged an interpreter? For deaf people, was having an interpreter the only way to communicate with the so called 'normal' human beings? Or could we put in a little extra effort in learning basic sign language to communicate with them? As I interviewed Murali, I realised how little effort it took to learn sign language.

Murali's story is beautiful because it has been told not through words, but straight from his heart. Murali's story is special because despite the apathetic attitude of people around him, Murali conquered all odds. Not only did his success open new doors for many like him, but also proved that even the sound of silence is powerful, provided it comes from deep within.

K. Murali was born in Coimbatore and was the fourth child in the family. His father was a district collector and mother, a housewife. His parents were both perfectly healthy. So when their second baby, a girl, was born deaf, the couple did not notice the child's handicap for long. They simply thought that she was one of those children who take a little extra time to respond. Never in their dreams did they think their little princess was born deaf and mute. It was only when their next child was born and started responding, but the elder one still did not, that they panicked. The doctors broke the news to them, silencing Murali's parents with their child's disability.

When Murali was born, his parents were more cautious and noticed Murali's unresponsiveness very early. Destiny had yet again played a cruel joke with the family. Two of their children had been born hearing and speech-impaired.

The couple loved all their children equally. The kids grew up together and got accustomed to their sibling's handicap. As Murali's sister (who was born healthy) puts it,

> *"As kids, we always wanted to communicate with each other. So we all picked up communication through sign language and lip-reading without any effort or lessons. In some sense, none of us needed formal sign language training to be able to communicate to each other."*

In the 1960s, education for deaf people was unheard of; not that the scenario is any better today. There is a big question mark on studies for the deaf and dumb. On the one hand, parents and society feel there is no need to educate these people when it is unlikely they'd get a good job. On the other, the few who come forward to study are not given admission in good schools. Employment is a big cause of concern. There are many jobs which the deaf can do. But corporate houses are sceptical to even give them a chance.

The deaf population of 1.1 million in India is 98% illiterate[1]. Yet, there are only around 500 schools which enrol the deaf in

---

[1]   http://en.wikipedia.org/wiki/Indo-Pakistani_Sign_Language

the country. How can we speak of equality and fairness in such a scenario?

Murali's parents were very keen on educating their children well. His father collected information from newspapers and paid visits to some schools around where they lived. But since there were no schools for the deaf in Coimbatore, his father got himself transferred to Thirunvelli and got Murali and his sister into a school for children with special needs.

The school adopted the oral method of learning. This method focuses on lip reading and then trying to make people speak/lip sync through a rigorous training by professionals.

For the uninitiated, there is a continuing debate in the deaf community between the two methods of communication; one through sign language and the other through oral learning. Murali is of the opinion that while oral learning can work for people who are partially deaf (up to thirty percent hearing loss), it does not work at all for people beyond a certain level of deafness (more than sixty percent hearing-impaired). He feels when a person has to struggle to utter words and his entire focus is on lip reading and trying to speak, how we can expect him or her to really communicate. Advocators of oral learning fail to see these issues. Their main aim is to induct the deaf and dumb into the mainstream.

Though their objective is noble, many like Murali feel it is practically stifling for hearing-impaired people and breaks their morale instead of boosting it. Forced by teachers to adopt oral learning, Murali lost interest in his studies and did not pursue his graduation. Finding a job was not easy either. His parents were very disappointed. Murali's father opened a tailoring shop for Murali so he could at least earn a living.

However, Murali played table tennis well and started representing India at various international events. As he had to travel frequently for various tournaments, he could not manage the shop and had to ultimately close it down. Murali then moved to Ooty where he worked for more than ten years in the dispatch department of Hindustan Photo Films. It was during this period that Murali got married to Sudha, who, like Murali, was hearing and speech impaired.

Murali and Sudha enjoy a perfectly harmonious relationship. However, when the time came to add a new member to the family, the couple had to go through various hardships. They worried whether their child would be born healthy or not. Murali's sister would accompany Sudha to the doctor and acted as an interpreter. In the absence of a trained medical personnel doing the interpretation between the doctor and the patient, Sudha had to go through many difficult situations. Little had the couple imagined that things could get worse. Sudha suffered from a medical complication and had two miscarriages. So while initially they worried whether their baby would be healthy, it now became a question of whether they could be parents at all.

All their prayers were answered when Sneha was born. To add to their joy, she was a perfectly healthy baby. Murali still remembers the feeling when Sneha responded to sounds and when she uttered her first words. In Sneha, the couple found a new hope. To make sure that Sneha had a healthy upbringing, Murali's mother stayed with them for the first couple of months.

And just like every child learns his mother tongue without any formal teaching, for Sneha, sign language became her mother tongue. She picked it up with much ease and without conscious efforts.

While he was working and leading a comfortable life, Murali always wished he could do something for the larger deaf and dumb community of which he was a part. He interacted with a lot of them and saw them struggling hard to make both ends meet. That is when he finally decided to do something about it.

In 2004, Murali and Sudha started a school with the aim of providing education to the deaf and dumb. The school was formally registered as 'Deaf Leaders'.

> "I had so much difficulty during my own education that my father had to get a transfer so that I could study. Not every parent is able to do that. There are hardly any schools in tier II and III cities which take deaf and dumb as students. So I wanted to ensure I could help others complete their education, at least basic education. I also wanted studying to be more fun and less strenuous. Students should not be pressurised into oral learning."

Deaf Leaders was completely self-funded to begin with. In the first batch of students, only four students were enrolled. Today, it runs two batches of twenty students each, providing them basic education and skills training completely free of cost. The organisation was started with the larger mission of bringing deaf people into the mainstream and it has lived up to its objective.

> "It was a great achievement for us when one student who had earlier failed twice in class X was able to pass after enrolling with us."

As the students started passing out of the school, there came the next challenge – the challenge of employability, of getting these people into relevant jobs. What would the students do with their education if at the end of the day, it could not get them their meals?

Through his network, Murali tried to get these students placed. Thus was born the next wing of Deaf Leaders.

> *"People need to be made aware of the capabilities of the speech and hearing-impaired people. They are bright and can work without interruptions and distractions. They tend to be very loyal employees and do not leave the organisations for a longer duration. Corporate houses have to be shown these benefits to convince them to hire these people. One of our students aspired to be a lecturer in a reputed college. We helped him complete his B. Com. and helped him get the post of assistant lecturer in Shankara Arts College. His students are very fond of him. What he cannot express through his words, he compensates with his knowledge."*

Murali's sincerity and dedication made this difficult task possible. Murali would sometimes personally accompany people to work to ensure they settled well in their new jobs, performed well and were not discriminated against. Deaf Leaders gave them all the basic skills training. Murali personally trained them to visit a bank and complete basic transactions. He instilled confidence in them and motivated them to take the first step towards success. As Murali rightly puts it,

> *"We make them true leaders of tomorrow."*

Of late, Murali has also been championing the cause of computer training for the hearing-impaired. At a time when the entire nation has been touched by the IT revolution, why should they be left behind? Imparting computer training will be a win-

win situation where the deaf and dumb can learn computers and take up jobs right from data entry to data analysis.

Over the last decade, Deaf Leaders has grown by leaps and bounds. After getting education and employment to the doorstep of the deaf fraternity, Murali has now started helping people find their life partners as well. The 'Deaf Matrimonial Chapter' of Deaf Leaders is another feather in Murali's cap.

> "Finding a right partner is very important for everyone. But for people who are deaf and dumb, it becomes critical because they can only truly express themselves to their life partners. They do not look at each other with pity. They understand each other's challenges well. So when it came to Deaf Leaders' next step, we thought of helping young men and women find their perfect life partners."

As it stands out today, the full form of the organisation's name, 'Deaf Leaders', encompasses all that it aims to achieve: 'Deaf Empowerment Activities for Literacy Education Accessible Development Employment Rehabilitation and Sports'.

It is an organisation working for the hearing and speech impaired, completely managed and run by the community itself.

Deaf Leaders has been continuously expanding its wings. Murali has been taking up various causes for the deaf and dumb. Right from organising the 'Deaf Expo' which celebrates the success of some prominent deaf achievers to organising silent film festivals. It has also hosted fashion shows by deaf and dumb models. Deaf Leaders has come a long way and has not just proved some of the myths plaguing our society wrong, but has also truly enabled and empowered disabled men and women. Deaf Leaders has made more than forty films focusing on the strengths, capabilities and achievements of the hearing and speech impaired people. Some of these movies have even bagged awards at national and international forums. The forum of the Deaf Expo showcases how the deaf and dumb are more capable than what the society generally believes them to be. All they need from society is support rather than neglect and sympathy.

"In the larger whole, our lives are intrinsically connected. In order for me to be truly happy and find meaning in my life, I have to serve others who need my help. That's the mission of my life, the purpose of my existence."

The volunteers associated with the organisation raise awareness about sign language among the society. The organisation organises drives where it reaches out to people and encourages them to learn basic sign language to communicate more easily with the deaf and dumb section of the society.

I now realise how easy it is to learn sign language. It is no rocket science. All you need is willingness to communicate. Specific professionals, especially doctors, police staff, and bank employees need to be especially trained to understand sign language. Sometimes tragedies occur when proper medical care is not provided to the deaf and dumb because of the inability of the doctors to understand what the patient intends to convey. Murali is presently working with a national university to develop a full-fledged course on sign language.

K. Murali has been invited to several international forums to give leadership training to the deaf people around the world. He has imparted training to hearing-impaired people in Japan, Sri Lanka, Malaysia, South Africa, Germany, France, UK, Singapore and many more countries. Many countries are impressed with the work Deaf Leaders is doing in India and have asked him to set up similar models in their nations. The world may be divided geographically but stands united when it comes to the voice of the disabled community.

In a society where we talk of social inclusion, we often miss out on the disabled community and their rights and concerns. Platforms like Deaf Leaders motivate people to move beyond their disabilities and add new significance to their existence.

Murali's never say die spirit, dedication and commitment towards the cause of disability is exemplified by a recent incident when he was approached by a few hotel management graduates who were unable to find a job for themselves.

"I approached a few restaurants to seek employment for them. But the perceptions that society has cannot be changed so easily. People said they do not want to employ hearing-impaired people, especially in the hospitality sector. I knew that if these myths had to be broken, we had to be the torch-bearers ourselves."

Deaf Leaders opened its very own restaurant. 365 D-café, as the restaurant is called, is completely run and managed by deaf and dumb people. Visitors come, order by either signalling at the menu or writing their order on a piece of paper. And the rest of the operations follow through smoothly. The second café opened in July 2013 and operates round the clock to provide food to more than 400 people every day.

D-café also reminds me of the Mirakle Courier Services which employs only the deaf and dumb people. Innovations like D-café and Mirakle should make us shed our pre-conceived notions that disabled people are not worth giving any opportunities to, while they have proved themselves time and again. To my mind, it's a question of our attitude more than their abilities or disabilities. I am sure, as long as people like Mr Murali exist, these myths will not have a long life.

Murali has won several laurels and awards, including the award for best social welfare, given by none other than the then Chief Minister of Tamil Nadu. But for Murali, the biggest award is the empowerment of so many lives around him, the Midas touch of Deaf Leaders.

> *"I am very happy when people smile from their heart. I will only rest when all my brothers and sisters are happy and satisfied."*

For the last eleven years, Murali has gone beyond his silence to give a voice to many others like him. From education to employment, and matrimony to entertainment, Murali has strived in all the realms of life to ensure justice for them. His actions definitely speak louder than words. It's time we start listening to the sound of silence.

Murali can be contacted at deafleaders@gmail.com.

Disability and Employment

Before I started writing this book, I often asked myself how and where the differently-abled people could be employed. When I found out that only 26 percent of the disabled people were employed and even less than 10 percent were employed in the formal sector, the statistics seemed obvious to me. What was the point of educating them if there were no suitable job opportunities to commensurate their education? Should we talk of education first and think about employment later? Or should we create an employment infrastructure and the education infrastructure would eventually follow? Doesn't it form a vicious circle?

It was only when I started my research on this topic that a hope filled my heart. I realised how non-disabled people often stereotype disabled people and think the disabled are incapable of anything. It was only after I met these dynamic people that I realised the limitations of my own thoughts. Not only have these people excelled in diverse fields of sports, arts, management, entertainment and social work, they have also made me realise the short-sightedness of my own vision.

Unfortunately, a lot of corporate HR personnel suffer from the same short-sightedness. Many said they would not recruit a differently-abled person at all. Most mentioned they have no policy for employment of such people. Only a few said that they would do a competency matching before taking a decision. And hardly a handful were true to their words and went on to recruit them. On many occasions, even those who recruit the differently-abled people underpay and exploit them on the pretext of disability.

During my interaction with the people in the book, I learned about the concept of job mapping for disabled people. I got to know that our policies also envisage provision for identification of jobs for the disabled community. Not just that, but with advancements in technologies, more and more jobs can now be brought under the umbrella of suitable jobs for the disabled.

For example, the job of a traffic policeman can easily be fit for a deaf person. In fact, he would be at an advantage, as he would be unaffected by the constant exposure to noise. I visited a beauty parlour which employed a blind girl, and have come across a courier company run exclusively by hearing-impaired staff. Data entry jobs can easily be done by someone physically handicapped. Autistic people can be trained to do jobs which are monotonous, the perfect example being a paper cup manufacturing factory where autistic people are involved in making thousands of paper cups and earning up to twenty thousand rupees a month while learning to be self-reliant in the process.

Many people interviewed in this book were refused jobs on the pretext of their disabilities. It was only after voicing their concerns to the government and media that they were given what they rightfully deserved. Since then they have all prospered in their professions. They have passed the most competitive exams, represented the country at national as well as international events, and are an important voice in our legislative structure.

The need of the hour is not to confine people but to create opportunities for them to come out of their homes. And the same is not just the responsibility of the government or the corporate houses; rather the entire society's.

So, next time, when you hear of a job opening, spend a minute to think if you could map that job to a differently-abled person. If you can, walk up to your company's HR and germinate the thought of employing someone to that job. Your smallest beginnings can make a significant difference in making this country disability-free, barrier-free.

Rajinder Johar:
Family of Disabled

I have fought with destiny to be alive;
To me, each day is God's present.
I may not have seen how the sun rises;
But I light the lives of thousands.

Shot at arm's length with bullets hitting his chest and spine, and rendered lifeless and immobile for more than twenty-eight years, Rajinder Johar's story is nothing short of a miracle. Until I met him, I could never contemplate that someone confined to his bed for so many years of his life, someone who has seen sunshine less than five times in all those years could lead a mission to serve an entire disabled community. Rajinder Sir is well-known, respected and in fact worshipped in the entire disabled fraternity.

His story brought tears to my eyes; tears of pride for a man who has never counted his sufferings but has kept a count of how many faces has he brought a smile on. Rajinder Sir's face glows with joy each time he tells me about his NGO's milestones and future plans. No words can do justice to his achievements. No matter how many inspirational speeches I may have listened to and how many motivational books I may have read, none has inspired me as much as the true story of this one man. I am all

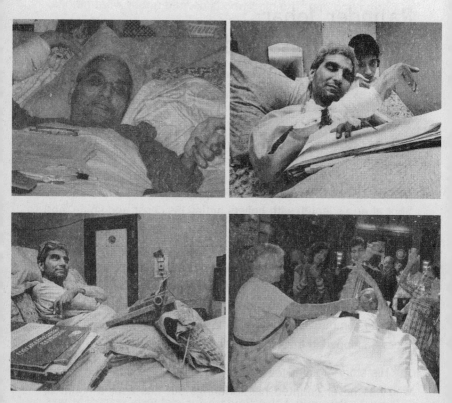

Disabled by a cruel quirk of fate, Rajinder Johar gathered his world and formed the 'Family of Disabled', now a leading organisation that provides help to make differently-abled people become self-sufficient.

ears to one of the greatest persons I have met in life. The man denied hope by doctors across the nation has given hopes to millions around him. The man who is defined not by what he has done for himself but for the difference he has brought in the lives of many others.

When I began my interview with Rajinder Sir, I was scared at the back of my mind. I expected a man who has been bed ridden for so long to be depressed, brooding over his fate. But the sight of a man lying still on a bed with a wide welcoming smile reminded me of my grandfather after he woke from his mid-day siesta. He welcomed me just like a grandfather would welcome his grandchildren from school, and that instantly put me at ease.

I started talking in Hindi, not sure if he was comfortable with English. But the moment, Rajinder Sir started talking, the fluency of his thoughts, the coherence of his words and the perfect English he speaks surprised me. The spark in his eyes left me spellbound. I was in awe of this man even before formally beginning the interview.

Rajinder Johar was born in Jalandhar and had been working as a senior occupational therapist at King George's Medical College, Lucknow in Uttar Pradesh for eighteen years. He was blessed with two children. Life was going on smoothly until the fateful day of 30 March 1986 when a robbery attempt at his house changed the family's life forever.

It was late in the evening. He had just returned home when three men knocked at the door and forced their way into his house. They pointed a gun at him. When the family tried to protest, one of them fired. In an attempt to save his family, Rajinder was hit by two bullets; one in the chest and one in the neck. The robbers fled assuming him dead.

Whether it was a case of robbery or a revengeful act, Rajinder Ji did not know. All he knew was that when he regained consciousness, he was crippled forever. After five months of treatment, the doctors declared that Rajinder was paralysed for life. His spine was permanently damaged and he would not be able to stand on his feet ever again. The lower half of his body was dead. In medical terms, he was now a quadriplegic.

From being the breadwinner of the family to being dependent on others even for his basic needs, life had taken the ugliest turn for him.

After being discharged from the hospital, his immediate concern was the family's finances. He had lost his job, so the family moved to Delhi, where Rajinder's father lived. His wife was working in a bank and got a transfer to Delhi.

"I felt lost, hopeless, and dejected."

The doctors told the family that quadriplegics do not live a long life. Their organs decay due to inactivity and soon fail. Quadriplegics usually lose their will to live because of loneliness and frustration too. The word the doctors used was not 'avoid' but 'delay'. They claimed the end was imminent, sooner or later. Hearing these words, Rajinder started waiting for his end.

"I felt as if I was of no use to anyone. Suddenly, pity replaced respect in people's eyes. It was better to die peacefully than leading such a dependent and disgraceful life. I was a burden on my family; both financially and emotionally. The doctors told my family that I needed regular physiotherapy

sessions, just to live. With our family's financial situation deteriorating, we could either spend money on my medical care or my children's education. I left my destiny to God and asked my father to get my children admitted into a good school."

Tough times continued for the family. Rajinder went through several mood swings. Thoughts of suicide would come often, but he forced himself come out of these for the sake of his children. He did not want his children to feel their father was a coward. His wife took on the entire family's responsibility and ensured their children did not have to leave their studies.

"Due to all these circumstances, my children lost their childhood much earlier. My son started taking care of me from a very young age. My daughter would come back from school and help me with my correspondence with the world outside. I would teach my children and narrate stories to them."

The children were very young when the incident had happened. They grew up seeing their father like this. They always complained to God for all that had happened.

Preeti Johar, Rajinder Ji's daughter says,

"As children, we would hate it when our father could not play with us, attend our parent-teacher's meetings. Unlike other children, we never went out on the weekends or family holidays. Our life was confined to our father's room. But because he was our teacher, we always looked up to him for everything."

Pankaj, his son also recollects similar childhood memories. He feared that if his friends knew about his father's condition, they might make fun of him. So, he started avoiding many of my friends and stayed alone lest they wanted to come home.

After surviving six long years of frustration, Rajinder finally resolved, "*Something will have to be done, or life will just continue without a purpose.*"

But what could a person who was bedridden do? How could a person who was dependent on others for all his needs even imagine doing something worthwhile? These were some of the questions society confronted Rajinder with. These were questions that plagued his mind as well.

> "*During the last eighteen years of my career, I had been a therapist; helping disabled people in my capacity as a doctor. So even though I was at the receiving end now, that is what I decided to do. Help disabled people.*"

But of course, nobody took him seriously. Everyone said, '*how will you manage?*' Rajinder thought a great deal about it and found a way to start. At that time, there was no magazine which voiced the concerns of disabled people. He decided to start one. He wanted to become the voice for the larger disabled family – a window to the outer world. It sounds easy to make such drastic decisions, but execution is a great challenge.

It was the constant motivation and assistance of his brother that sailed him through the difficult times. Right from changing his dressings every 3-4 days to designing a writing device for him, Surinder has always been there for his brother. Despite having his own family responsibilities, he would spend a lot of his evenings by Rajinder's side. Surinder also designed a simple water bottle and a mechanism where neither would Rajinder have to depend on anyone for as basic a need as drinking water. They were simple things but they changed Rajinder's life for the better.

"Through his efforts, he made life easier for me. If you see me alive today, my brother, Surinder has a huge role to play in it. It was because of my brother that I finally decided to push myself out of depression and start living.

"In fact, the first thousand rupees for setting up 'Voice' came from my brother's pocket. Surinder is a man of few words, but a saint at heart. I am happy it all started with a saint's money. Maybe, that's the reason why it has paid the dividends in the long run."

Rajinder Ji gave out an advertisement on cable TV saying that he needed volunteers to start this magazine. Help poured in.

"There were two volunteers who joined me in my cause. One was a young girl who wanted to put in two hours every day for this magazine. Another was an elderly lady who came forward to help."

In 1992, with a two-member team, the first edition of the magazine came out. The magazine was titled 'Voice' signifying that it was the voice of disabled people. But the question remained on how the entire project would be funded.

God showed the path ahead. In one television programme, Rajinder saw an artist, Shivani Gupta who was wheelchair bound. He got in touch with her. She was a painter and was ready to give her designs for printing greeting cards. But the difference would be that these greeting cards were to be made by disabled people. In the first print run, they printed about three thousand greeting cards. The entire lot was soon sold out. The volunteers at the organisation worked on improving the designs. All the cards were designed and painted by disabled people. Thus, with the profits from selling the cards, 'Voice' was funded.

As work expanded, he hired a managing editor for the magazine. But the editor's shoddy work led to a sudden collapse of the magazine's readership, making it infeasible to print the magazine anymore. Efforts are still on to revive it. It was an important lesson for Mr. Johar. Different people would form the backbone of all his efforts and who worked with the project could either make or break the entire initiative.

Despite the failure, the fire to do something for the disabled fraternity remained with him. With baby steps, Rajinder formally registered the Family Of Disabled (FOD) to find newer ways of helping disabled people in need. Rajinder chose the name to clearly signify the values and ideals of the organisation. It was not a random group being christened, but a family.

He personally wrote to Mother Teresa, seeking her blessings. When her second in command signed the letter and sent it back, Rajinder Ji wrote back humbly seeking a letter from the holy mother herself. Finally, he received a letter from her, blessing FOD.

"I knew now I could not fail. I had the blessings of the holy mother."

In 1996, FOD reached its first milestone when it started distributing aids and appliances to the disabled people free of cost. Right from donating wheelchairs, tricycles, crutches, walking sticks, and hearing aids to others, FOD continues to donate need-specific gadgets like reading telescopes, bicycles, etc. The objective of this service was and is to try and make life easier for many people and provide them much needed support for becoming independent.

> "We always wish to do something different from what the other NGOs are already doing for the disabled community. It is necessary to donate what people need and not what we want to donate. Last year, we donated I-pods to blind girls. They needed it to record lectures in college. We have even donated adult diapers to people in need. Till date, 1032 people have benefitted under this project."

I am surprised that Rajinder Ji remembers the exact number of beneficiaries. But then, each life is important and worth counting.

Employability is one of the biggest challenges for the disabled people. FOD started getting a lot of requests from people, asking if they could help them set up a small shop and the like. Initially, FOD helped on a case-to-case basis. But soon, Rajinder decided to make it a regular endeavour of FOD. In 1998, FOD started the Apna Rozgaar Scheme. As the name indicates, this scheme aims at self-employment for disabled people. The project aimed at giving five thousand rupees in kind as an interest-free loan to disabled people to start the trade of their choice.

> "Whether someone wants to start a tea stall or become a cobbler, we give him/her all the raw material. Till date, we have helped close to seven hundred people start more than forty different kinds of occupations. We have never forced them to choose any particular occupation. We are mere

facilitators. If someone succeeds, he returns the money and can again take a loan anytime in future. The project has a 75% success rate, while 25% people abscond. But we cannot stop giving a new life to 75% people just because 25% broke our trust."

In a society where disabled people are underpaid, such a project is bringing smiles on the faces of many.

FOD resolved to pick a new initiative every three years and find new ways to help the needy people. With the help of his brother, Rajinder Ji conceptualised a bigger roadmap for FOD. He would plan while others executed. The good thing was that more and more people started getting associated with FOD and were pleased to give a platform to his vision.

In 2001, FOD started a project called Beyond Limits. Under this project, disabled artists showcased their work in an annual art exhibition. Their work is auctioned and the money collected is directly given to the artists. As many as 120 artists have been able to participate in these exhibitions.

"The way directors in the film industry say they have given break to an actor, I can proudly say FOD has given a break to these artists. The more meaning I add to people's lives, the more meaningful I find my own existence."

A very deep thought and a very positive one; couldn't the world's problems be solved if each of us thought like that? How we waste almost our entire lives trying to find the meaning of life, but with our thought process concentrated just on our own existence, we hardly succeed. But then that's what makes Rajinder Ji so special.

Project Gyan Path was started in the year 2006. FOD started helping disabled people attain education and also enroll in various professional courses. FOD would take care of all the expenses of their education, right from nursery to post-graduation. Rajinder Ji's face lights up as he mentions that some of the beneficiaries have completed their B. Ed. and are now teachers, imparting the gift of education to many more students.

> *"Gyan Path means the road to knowledge. We have enabled more than seventy students to move on this road and become educated. We have helped them study in best-in-class private institutions, never compromising on their dreams and aspirations. Each time a student moves ahead in life, I feel I am worthy of living."*

While Rajinder is engrossed in telling me all about FOD, I am puzzled. Who is the force behind it? Where do the finances come from? How is Rajinder so involved in these projects? In front of me lies a man who cannot even move from his bed. But the spark in his eyes, the excitement and pride in his voice seems to defy all these limitations.

Sensing my impatience, Rajinder Ji finally answers the question that has been bothering me for some time now.

> *"We have no government funding. One needs to run hard to get government funding; something I definitely cannot do.*
>
> *"To be honest, each time we launched a project, this question would arise. Where would the money come from? But each time, God has been great. We have found exceptional voluntary support. People see the work we do, the transparent systems we have in place and are willing*

to contribute. We have found sponsors who have stayed on with us for years. Apart from this, we also collect waste material from different places across Delhi, make stuff out of it and sell the same to make some money. We have also found sponsors like the Bank of America, HSBC, Amex who have bought stuff made by disabled people"

All this is incredible. So much so, that if I had not personally met Mr. Rajinder, I would not have believed such miracles can happen. A man who has not seen the light of the day for almost three decades has given a bright future to an extended family.

"All this gives me immense pleasure. Doing nothing was taking me nowhere. But now, I sleep in peace."

Rajinder Johar and FOD have collectively bagged twenty-one awards, including two national awards, even though Rajinder Sir can hardly step out of his room, forget attending these award functions. Nevertheless, the biggest award for him has been the million smiles he has brought to the world. He is adored by people even remotely connected to FOD. For people who work directly with him, he is a messiah – a pure soul.

The entire organisation is now managed by Preeti, Rajinder Ji's daughter.

Preeti feels proud of her father as she says,

"I have always looked up to my father. Right from being my teacher in childhood, to being my mentor, my father is my leader, my inspiration and my hero. My father plans, while my team (which comprises eleven people and many volunteers) and I execute his ideas."

Did Preeti voluntarily get into FOD?

"Well, yes and no. FOD has been my father's baby. But seeing so many disabled people throng our house everyday had definitely made me more sensitive to their needs. There were and are times when my father has fallen terribly sick. Even a normal cough makes his condition critical. His organs which have grown so weak cannot sustain any infection. But on all such occasions, my father was not worried of his own health but about what would happen to FOD and the people dependent on it. My brother was engrossed in taking care of father's medical needs and so could not pay much attention to FOD. I slowly got involved in it. FOD is a big responsibility. Till date, my father says I still have a lot to learn. He is training me. Only when he feels 100 percent confident will he give me full charge of FOD."

Preeti has a family of her own. How does she manage? Preeti smiles,

"I did not want to get married. I wanted to dedicate my entire life to FOD. It was only when my husband assured me that he would support me in all my endeavours did I convince myself to get married. My in-laws are very supportive and encouraging. They see the work FOD is doing and are proud of it."

Pankaj shares the same feelings.

"It is the strong Indian family roots which have kept us together. We all have a shared dream. FOD is a family.

How can we let it go? We do not know how long dad will be around, but this is his family; our family. We will always find him in FOD."

Pankaj has made a documentary on his father, titled *Standing Still*. This documentary has won several accolades and awards. The one hour film beautifully captures Rajinder Ji's victory over all odds. One of the senior members of Aamir Khan Productions saw the documentary and went to tell Aamir Khan about it.

Rest as they say is history. FOD was one of the two organisations from disability sector which were featured in actor Aamir Khan's TV reality show *'Satyamev Jayate'* (Season 1) on 10 June 2012. After the show Aamir Khan thus appealed to the general public,

"Family Of Disabled is doing a wonderful job by helping many disabled people. I would like more and more people from all over India to come forward and support FOD financially so that they are able to continue and expand their good work." —Aamir Khan

Following the episode, viewers poured their hearts out and offered tremendous support to FOD. With society's generous contributions, FOD is constructing a multi-purpose rehabilitation centre called Unnati for persons with disabilities in Najafgarh, New Delhi.

"Call it God's wish or our destiny, whenever we are short of funds, help flows in from unexpected quarters."

FOD's journey has been miraculous. From not having enough to bear his own expenses to having such a happy and growing family, Rajinder Ji has proved that there is no limit to dreaming. People like him are truly inspirational. I hope that the prayers of his family do not go unanswered.

"I believe that family is the best rehabilitation centre for any individual. Having worked at a hospital for so long, I know that paid care at the hospital is meaningless compared to selfless care of the family."

The people who conspired to kill him have all died. But Rajinder Ji has survived not just the two bullets but twenty-eight years of stillness to expand his family.

"It is God's decision. When I see people around me fulfilling their dreams, I feel happy. God has given me the responsibility of so many lives. He would not call me before I fulfil those."

Rajinder Ji has taught me the most important lesson of my life. He has taught me that happiness is found in not just living for oneself but for making a difference to the world, despite one's own limitations.

I come across a paper in the Indian Journal of Occupational Therapy authored by Rajinder Sir. It talks about advantages of quadriplegia, how it has helped him expand his circle of well-wishers, minimised his needs to buy shoes and made him the apple of everyone's eye; a very light yet brave hearted attempt to regard a life threatening challenge as an advantage.

As I end the conversation, I am numb.

I text Preeti, *"Rajinder Uncle is an angel."* He truly is.

How far can you go if you are not mobile? Rajinder Ji teaches us that there is no limit. Your courage and willpower can defy all odds.

Even when the world has written you off, you are the captain of your soul, the master of your destiny.

Rajinder Ji can be contacted at rajinderjohar@gmail.com.

Disability and Attitudinal Barriers

Consider a mother whose child cannot see. Does she need to be reminded of it? Consider a father whose child cannot walk. Does he need to be made to feel more burdened?

How many of us have looked at disabled people not with sympathy or pity, but with respect? How many of us have given a few rupees to a disabled beggar on the street and have felt satisfied to have done our bit? How often have we discouraged our children to play with a boy or girl in the neighborhood who is crippled? Have we ever recommended a disabled person for a job, despite knowing that technically he would be fit and competent? How often have we thought about, leave aside accepting, a marriage between a differently-abled and a non-disabled person?

A lot of people feel that disability is a curse, often determined by our past actions. I have also heard people go to the extent of saying that disability is a way of God's punishment. It is ironical then that polio has been eradicated from the country. Have our past actions become purer? Or has God become more merciful? How can people even get the thought of God taking revenge or punishing in their minds? Something surely is terribly wrong here.

A lot of the characters in the book had faced social stigma with their own friends and relatives abandoning them, telling them how their lives were over, how they were a burden for their parents, and de-motivating them from seeking a purpose to their lives. This not only has a negative impact on differently-abled people but also on their families.

I have read shocking incidences where parents have killed their own child simply because they were too scared of the future of an 'incapable' child. Incidences of rape of mute girls have shaken my soul. One of the persons in the book, Suresh, was robbed in broad daylight at one of the country's busiest railway stations with no one coming forward to help him. To what extent can the society be apathetic, cold and even devilish? Isn't the silent spectator to all this as much a culprit as the criminal himself?

While the physical barriers can be overcome by policy changes, no big revolution can be brought about unless there is a change in the attitude of people towards the disabled community. It needs no government intervention, it needs no policy changes, and it needs no technological advancements. All it needs is a little compassion, sensitivity and love. And a little humanity amongst us.

The journey to change a dysfunctional social thought process would be a long one. Typically, society indulges in the habit of what is called 'generalisation of failure and individualisation of success'. This means whenever a differently-abled is successful, society categorises it as an 'exception'. On the other hand, whenever the same person is not successful, it is termed as a 'rule'. In order to break this pattern, there is a need for change within each one of us. Disabled people need no special schools, no reservations and no quotas. They, in fact, crave to be treated as one amongst us, without any sympathy or special treatment. They just need friends and well wishers.

Sheela Sharma:
Hands Off! It's All about the Feet

Nature is beautiful, for those who care to observe;
Life is full of colours, for those who wish to live.
Love is beautiful, for those who have experienced it.
Disability can be an opportunity too, for those who set themselves free.

Often as we grow up, we recollect memories of our childhood; of playing in the mud, dancing in the rains, running around with friends, and being loved and pampered by our parents. Memories which make us smile and make us want to become a child again. But not everyone is fortunate to have a healthy childhood. For some, the disharmony in their parent's relationship makes the memories of their childhood haunting. Sheela Sharma's childhood was a dark period. Her mother had jumped onto the railway track with Sheela in her arms. With a train hurtling at her at full speed, Sheela's mother was killed, but Sheela survived, albeit destined to a dark future. Losing both her arms in the accident, Sheela went on to live a dark and hopeless life. But life turned colourful again when Sheela was introduced to the world of painting. Sheela learnt to express herself through her work and is now one of the most prominent foot and mouth artists of the country. Her story is about a person battered by life from all corners and still finding a way to live, to smile. The story of her left foot is the story of the triumph of spirit.

Sheela lost her arms in an accident, but trained herself diligently to paint using her left foot. She paints on women issues and her colours make so many lives wonderful and hopeful.

Sheela was born in Gorakhpur and had one of the most difficult childhoods one could imagine. At a time when other children played happily with their parents, Sheela would see hers fighting and quarrelling. Sometimes the abuses they hurled at each other made her wonder why they did not end their marriage. Was poverty the curse or her father's habit of drinking, Sheela did not know. All she craved was love and peace.

On that unfortunate day Sheela's father hurled abuses at her mother again. Fed up of the abuses and of being beaten up, Sheela's mother could take it no more. She did not know what to do and where to go.

Frustrated, she lost her will to live and in a fit of rage, decided that the solution to her troubles was death. She decided to end her life. While it is difficult to speculate what could have gone on within her, what she did was definitely unimaginable. Perhaps she did not want to leave her child at the mercy of the big bad world. Perhaps she feared that with her gone, Sheela would have no future. So she decided to kill her daughter before taking her own life. She decided that along with her, her daughter would have to leave the world.

Holding her little girl to her chest, she jumped in front of a train. In the blink of an eye, her body was shred into pieces. Sheela had a miraculous escape but both her arms had to be amputated. Her future was thrown into darkness. Orphaned, disabled and with nowhere to go, life seemed bleak for the little girl.

"When I opened my eyes, I was in pain. As a child, I could not understand what was happening around me. I noticed the amputation but thought maybe I was hallucinating under the heavy doses of medicines. Someone left me at a boarding school for the disabled in Delhi. I sometimes think it might have been my very own father. I do not remember."

Traumatic recollections troubled her. Often she would wake up sweating in the middle of the night. Whenever she would come across a railway track, she would feel her feet were frozen.

"As I grew up, I no longer wanted to live. I had horrific memories of the incident always coming back to haunt me."

For the little girl, her existence itself was a big question mark. She had lost her mother and her father had abandoned her. She grew up without hands and had no choice but to learn to do all her daily chores using her feet. Right from changing clothes to having food, Sheela had to do everything using her feet. Life offered her no other choice.

A chance encounter with a disabled arts teacher in the boarding school gave her the first exposure to the world of painting. The artist gave Sheela elementary lessons making her hold the brushes with her foot.

As a child, when she saw her teacher paint, Sheela would feel drawn towards the colours. The world of painting was a no-barred world, where she could paint freely and express herself. It was a world which took her away from her painful memories. It was a medium to express the silent sufferings in her life. It was a canvas to begin afresh. All this inspired Sheela to put in extra effort to learn the art of painting using her foot.

It came after a lot of practice and many challenges. Each time Sheela tried to hold brushes with her foot and it didn't work, and each time she tried to paint fine lines ending up painting a stroke wrong, Sheela resolved to try harder.

"The day I was able to hold a brush steady and complete a painting with my foot was perhaps the happiest day of my life."

She started by painting large blocks but soon trained herself to paint finer paintings. Sheela would find excuses to paint and would gift her paintings to her friends and teachers in school. It was the beginning of a new phase in her life. But just when she had begun to settle in her new world, life again took a turn. The boarding school she was in was abruptly shut down. Sheela was put in a government's women's protection home in Lucknow.

This separation from her arts teacher was a big blow to her. Just when she felt she had found a reason to be happy, all was lost. Nevertheless, the fire had been ignited within her. She resolved that even the worst of circumstances could not take away her deep desire to train herself to paint. There was no money for any formal training. Thus Sheela knew that self training would be the only solution if she really wanted to achieve something.

The world of painting was a place where she had the liberty to shape things, colour things as per her imagination. Be it the pain of being disabled or of being orphaned, Sheela felt her deepest sorrows dissolve in the strokes of her brushes. This new found skill made her confident and kept her motivated. It set her free.

People who came to the protection home expressed their sympathies but never encouraged her. People found the idea of foot painting strange and even told her that she couldn't continue to paint this way in a sustainable manner. People would discourage her and tell her that painting would not take her anywhere. But Sheela took everything in her stride and fought against all odds.

"Most people who visit such orphanages come there with a sympathetic attitude towards its inmates. They can feed us for a day. But they never think of their responsibilities beyond that. Shouldn't they look at a larger role of aligning us with mainstream society, of helping us become independent? Children in such orphanages are not looking for chocolates,

they could do better with books. They do not want to be dependent on others. Rather, they want others to help them become independent."

There were occasions when she would feel like giving up. She saw no hope in life. Her courage would begin to fade and she would feel restless. But her strong will and commitment to learn helped her conquer all the challenges.

"Essentially, there was no option for me. My mother had committed the sin of suicide. I did not want to follow suit. It was the call of my soul. Painting was my identity which I did not want to give up."

Sheela consciously trained her left foot to paint. As she grew up, so did her desire to become an accomplished artist. She applied to the Lucknow Arts College.

"I still remember how I craved to get admission in the Arts College. I thought I won't be able to qualify the test, yet I appeared for it."

Sheela was so pessimistic that she didn't even check the admission results for a week. Then, one day, as she casually walked into the college, people started congratulating her. It was then that she got to know that she had not just got admission but had in fact, had topped the entrance test. Her joy knew no bounds.

Sheela wanted to pursue her interest in fine arts. As the name suggest, fine arts is less commercialised and allows a free flow of art; whereas commercial art is more tuned towards the commercial demands of the society and severely constraints an artist aesthetically. But a squabble between the teachers of commercial and fine arts forced her to take up commercial art. Perhaps the teachers wanted to commercialise her disability.

Till that point, Sheela had never bothered about the technicalities of painting. She painted more from her heart than getting lost in technical details. Thus, though she obtained a degree in commercial arts, she never found herself truly immersed in it. It was a newfound dilemma for Sheela and created more confusion and self doubt.

With her education complete, she went to exhibit her paintings regularly at the Lalit Kala Academy, Lucknow. Her paintings got instant recognition and made her a celebrated name in the field of arts in a short span of time.

Through her paintings, Sheela brings alive the joy as well as the challenges of womanhood. Most of her work is centred on that theme. Her paintings are a reflection of her journey – her pain and struggle. Sheela also paints nature in its true beauty, free of shackles. Birds are especially close to her heart as they signify freedom to her. Drawn with innocence, her figures often evoke feelings close to divinity.

In the last fifteen years, Sheela's paintings have found a place at many reputed art galleries and exhibitions all across the country. Besides several cultural awards, Sheela has also received a national award for her spirit from none other than Maneka Gandhi.

Sheela got married in 2005. The story of her matrimony is an equally inspiring one. Sudheer, her husband, is a sculptor and both of them share a common passion towards art. They both met in the Lucknow Arts College and a great bond of friendship struck. Sudheer was touched by Sheela's zeal and will power. When he visited her in the women's home, he was touched by the way she did all her work with her feet. The two developed a mutual feeling of love and respect, but both were too apprehensive of expressing it. Finally, Sheela proposed and Sudheer gladly accepted. Sudheer feared his mother's reaction on this so called 'unequal' relationship and did not tell his mother of their marriage for almost a year, before a local newspaper carried a story on the couple. But contrary to his fears, his mother was proud of his choice and welcomed Sheela with open arms. Their union is one of deep love and respect for each other's talent.

> *"We have had many challenging moments but our love has helped us overcome these. My mother-in-law in particular has been a pillar of strength for me. Her love has given me the love of a mother and has been my greatest strength in recent times."*

Sudheer's love made him see through Sheela's disability to find a perfect life partner. In this world where we read of wives being harassed for dowry, Sudheer and Sheela's love is inspirational.

The couple is blessed with two children and is leading a life of harmony.

> *"I feel my life has come full circle. Abandoned by my parents, I wish to shower a lot of love on my children. My husband and I want to ensure a happy life for them – one where childhood blooms and blossoms."*

Sheela could have died along with her mother, but she was destined to live. Sheela could have succumbed to beggary but she was destined to paint. Sheela could have been alone but she was destined to be a mother. From being a nobody in the crowd to this stage where she is not only independent but also a well-known artist, Sheela has come a long way. Her commitment, strong resolve, desire to achieve and fighting spirit have helped Sheela achieve the impossible. Sheela has proven that there is no barrier to anything you desire. It is your passion that takes you forward.

Sheela can be contacted at sheelaartist@gmail.com.

Disability and Marriage

It is often said that marriages are made in heaven. Often, girls dream of their knight in shining armour and guys dream of their queens. Parents too dream of a good life partner for their children. Do these dreams and hopes change if one is differently-abled? Does being visually-impaired make you unsuitable for someone with perfect vision? Can two deaf people marry and live happily? What if you get married and then you or your partner becomes disabled?

Questions like these are too personal to be asked. But the more I talked to the people mentioned in this book and the more they opened to me, I took the liberty to ask them some of these sensitive questions. I met George who was visually impaired but his wife was not. The couple has been happily married for more than two decades. I met Mr Murali whose wife was deaf as well but they had a perfectly healthy relationship. Sheela's husband loved her for the beauty of her soul, and looked beyond her handicap to fall in love with her. Today, they have been married for almost a decade and beautifully complement each other.

I met a girl who was genetically disabled. She often told me how she wanted to marry someone who was not disabled. Her point of view was that if both of them would be suffering, who would take care of them and eventually they both would spend a frustrated life with multiple hospital visits. And yet, the cruel fact was that non-disabled men often took advantage of her. Eventually, as destined, she fell in love with a guy who had the same disability as her. And the fact of the matter is that both of them are more appreciative of each other's needs and understand each other to a greater extent than any other guy or girl would have. They just completed a year of togetherness and look forward to many more.

I also met a girl who had been affected by polio and had married a guy who proposed his love for her. While he spoke of his love and made her believe in love, just ten days into their marriage, he realised the practical implications of that relationship. The end result was a life of abuse, agony and regrets for the girl.

I met Neeru who has remained unmarried out of choice. For she feels that if she needs two caretakers to even move her from her bed to her wheelchair, marriage does not make much sense. She would prefer to spend her life in the company of her friends, rather than getting married.

None of these choices is wrong or right in the absolute sense. Marriages and relationships are a matter of personal choice and should be left at that. But one lesson which is common in all such cases is that if you are someone marrying a disabled person, whether or not you are disabled yourself, you need to be appreciative of the person's needs and limitations upfront, rather than realising them at a later stage in life when all that is left is pain, agony and frustration. One must remember that relationships are successful and beautiful, beyond the differentiation and classification of someone who has a disability.

Jay Chhaniyara:
Laugh away all your worries

In today's world of jealousy and competition;
Laughter is expensive and hard to share.
Laughter though is my mission and gift to the world;
Laughter though is my prayer.

Most of us feel that life is full of tensions, struggles and competition. In this journey, we seldom smile. Only a few of us really laugh our hearts out without any inhibitions. We leave that job to a comedian. Years ago, the movie *Mera Naam Joker* depicted a joker's life. It showed how, despite the troubles in his own life, the joker made people laugh. Years later, when comedy shows became a rage on television, a child became a household name. A boy who suffers from cerebral palsy and is wheelchair-bound is making the world forget all their worries and laugh aloud. Jay's life is an everyday struggle. At the age of twenty, Jay has undergone more than twenty operations and has spent the prime of his life in hospitals.

Kudos to Jay for hiding all his pain as he sets out to make people smile and forget their worries. As he says, *"laughter is the best medicine."*

When I first told Jay about the book, his first question was, *"Would the book be of any benefit to the disabled people?"*

Crippled in body by cerebral palsy, Jai is happier in spirit for he makes others laugh. He is a well-known comedian and has been a part of numerous TV shows.

On hearing that it would be, Jay agreed to give an interview right away, without any further questions; a gesture which speaks volumes about the purity of his soul.

Jay Chhaniyara was one of the twins born to Deepak and Heena Chhaniyara in October 1993 in Rajkot, Gujarat. Born premature, the twins did not cry when born. One of the twins died the very next day. After days of battling with death, the other one survived. His parents thus christened the baby, 'Jay' (which means 'victory' in Hindi).

For a whole year, Jay's parents could not understand why their child could not put a grip on things. His brain had not grown fully. Jay was diagnosed to be suffering from cerebral palsy. Despite undergoing several physiotherapy sessions, Jay could not walk and would often fall down. The sessions were painful for the little one and were soon discontinued when they bore no results.

Meanwhile, his parents got him admitted to a nearby school, but the school did not take responsibility of Jay's care. His school authorities insisted that one of his parents should always stay with him in school, lest something happens. Jay's condition worsened as he grew up. Soon he could no longer walk and his education was discontinued.

Many doctors were consulted, temples visited. But nothing seemed to be working. The family was losing hope. It was the most painful period for Jay's parents. Jay's father was a government servant and got a meagre salary. Most of the expenses for Jay's treatment were met by taking loans. Financially and emotionally, the family was devastated.

When Jay was six years old, he had to undergo surgeries on both his legs to release the convulsions developed in his muscles. Recuperating at home after the operation, Jay was in pain. To cheer him up, his elder brother gifted him an audio cassette of jokes. Later in the evening when Jay's friends came to visit him, Jay narrated the entire cassette to them.

"This is Side A. Now listen to Side B!"

Everyone around him was spellbound. How could a six year old child memorise an entire audio cassette after listening to it only once? For the first time, the family realised how gifted their child was. That was the first glimpse of his ability.

Jay had found a new passion in life. Comedy was to become his saviour, his medicine.

"If I had to survive, I had to laugh away my pain and make others laugh."

Whenever anyone would come home to enquire about his health and meet the 'patient', Jay ensured the person walked out not with pity but with a smile on his face. He started doing mimicry acts during family get-togethers. From being a child who was pitied upon and avoided, Jay became the most sought after person at all neighbourhood events. Jay's first formal comedy show was in a community celebration during Navratri, where he was applauded by the entire community.

Soon Jay became popular in the entire Gujarati community. Word of mouth referrals got l   many more local shows. Jay auditioned for a comedy show on ETV Gujarat, a regional channel. His appearance on that channel made him a household name in Gujarat.

His parents were only too happy that Jay was busy and that his mind was diverted from his own pain. They encouraged him to do what he enjoyed. In fact his mother would accompany him wherever he wanted to go and perform.

In 2004, at the age of eleven, Jay went to Mumbai for his treatment. As luck would have it, he came to know of a competition called '*Koi Bhi Aao – Hansa ke Dikhao*'. The competition was telecasted on Sahara One. At that time, Jay was not very fluent in Hindi. To add to that, there were more than 750 participants of all age groups and from different parts of the country. But Jay decided to take up the challenge.

> *"People would look at me and question my abilities. Instead of being dejected by their negative comments, I became even more determined in my endeavours."*

Not only did Jay perfect his Hindi in just two days, he went on to win the competition. The reward of fifty thousand rupees and a Hollywood trip with his family lifted his spirits. When the show was telecast, his talent was spotted by Mr Shekhar Suman, the famous Indian TV artist. Later, when Shekhar Suman was invited to be a judge at *The Great Indian Laughter Challenge*, he invited Jay to perform on the show. After this show, Jay Chhaniyara became a national rage.

Jai's maiden performance on national television left many eyes moist. Post his performance, Shekhar Suman commented, "*He is not sitting on a wheelchair. It is a will chair.*"

Jai's performance won him many hearts. Since then, Jai has been performing at various national and international shows. Despite having no formal education, Jay has learnt Hindi and English solely by hearing others speak. His jokes have made him a household name in the country. But behind all this is a person who has undergone more than twenty surgical operations in his life. His body develops convulsions and his hands and legs get twisted. Not a week goes by when he does not have to go for physiotherapy.

His life is either spent doing comedy shows or in hospitals. Jay has seen immense pain in life. But there is a famous saying, "Do you want to be a humorist? Where are your tears?" Jay has resolved to take away pain from others' lives. That has come to be the objective of his life.

Jay's father has a spark in his eyes as he says,

"Our entire family supports him. Today our entire family is known and respected across the world, all thanks to Jay."

Yet Jay is only a child. His body is weak and he falls sick very often. Often he gets scared by loud sounds. There are times when people laugh at him. There are times when fear grips him. There are times when he panics and forgets all he has learnt. But he never gives up, nor does his family.

Jay is on a mission to eradicate the miseries of the world through the medicine of laughter. He does not want people's pity; he has earned respect for himself. He feels that talking about his sufferings makes him even more vulnerable. He says,

"जीने का मतलब मैंने मोहब्बत में पा लिया,
जिसका भी गम हुआ उसे अपना लिया,
आप रो कर भी गम को हल्का न कर सके,
मैंने हंसी की आड़ में हर गम को छुपा लिया"
(I have taken the pain from the lives of others, hiding my pain behind laughter.)

Jay feels that the world can be made a better place if only people learn to laugh heartily. *"No one can be bad if they can laugh heartily."*

Anyone in Jay's place would complain to God. But Jay has great faith in God and has recorded several hymns in his own voice.

Jay says,

"जिसने ये क़ायनात बनाई है, उस पर भरोसा नहीं करेंगे तो किस पे करेंगे?"
(If you would not trust the creator of this world, whom would you?)

Millions of blessings and his faith in God have finally begun to bear fruit. In 2012, Jay underwent another major surgery at Allahabad. After seven months of rehabilitation and intensive care, Jay has started walking using sticks.

Jay's journey on the road of laughter has given him more than 1500 shows and appearances in more than 25 TV shows all across the globe. He has also been conferred with several eminent awards by government bodies, clubs and associations, the media and entertainment industry. His creative skills have been lauded by several eminent personalities. Once Jay met Sachin Tendulkar in a hotel. Post the meeting, Sachin said, *"He is not challenged; he is ready for all the challenges."*

Aamir Khan beautifully described Jay's contribution to the world when he said, *"Happiness is the only thing which a person can give to others even if he does not have it. And you are doing the same."*

He smiles and says, *"My father was a government employee. Owing to my huge medical expenses, money has been a constraint for our family. So whenever I win an award, I am happy that we have some extra savings for the month. Getting an award is of immense help to me, but my biggest reward is the appreciation I get from everyone, especially the smiles on other's faces."*

Jay has created a dedicated trust for helping disabled people and 50 percent of his income goes into this trust. From these funds, Jay donates aids and appliances to disabled people. He wants to encourage others like him to rise above their disabilities. He ends the conversation with a message for them.

"मंज़िल का रास्ता ऐसे तय हो गया है,
के अब पर्वत को भी मुझसे भय हो गया है,
पैदा होते ही जिन हाथों पे पराजय लिखा गया था,
वो आज घिस घिस कर "जय" हो गया है।"
(My determination has shaken mountains. The defeat in my fate is now translating into success.)

Jay can be contacted at laughwithjay@gmail.com.

Divya Arora:
Bas itni si guzaarish...

Pretty woman with a heart of gold;
Living in her dream world and fantasies.
Standing at the cliff, she watches the sunset;
Waiting for the man of her dreams.

I was awed by Hrithik Roshan's heartrending role of a quadriplegic in the movie *Guzaarish*, but never put a thought to the kind of training Hrithik must have gone through to give such a convincing performance. Never did I think of the person who would be behind Hrithik's flawless performance.

Then I met Divya, a lively young lady who was not just Hrithik's trainer for the film but also a living inspiration for him. A child artist who was handpicked by Bollywood, her destiny pulled her into the film industry ever since she was child, albeit this child could not stand on her feet.

Divya has been suffering from cerebral palsy since her birth. But that has not stopped her from being Bollywood's darling. From being an actor to being a script writer, from being a girl-next-door to Miss India runner up (in special category), this girl is a storehouse of energy. Her smile will make you smile as will her beautiful eyes

161

Divya was not just Miss India runner up in special category, she is also now a director and script writer. She was the trainer behind Hrithik Roshan's flawless performance in Guzaarish and continues to spread joy through her active theatre and Bollywood network.

which cannot hide her dreams and innocence. Read on to know how Divya has overcome all the obstacles in her path to lead a life worthy of respect and admiration. Read her *guzaarish* to life.

In the beautiful moments of child birth, Divya's mother had no clue her daughter would grow up to be a cerebral palsy patient; a disease which would put her daughter on a wheelchair for the rest of her life.

It was only when Divya could not walk even at the age of two that her parents first consulted doctors, who after few a physiotherapy sessions referred her case to the All India Institute of Medical Sciences. At AIIMS, the doctors first diagnosed her disability.

As like any other parents, Divya's parents also wanted to see their baby take her first steps. But Divya would just not make an effort to move around. Her parents would tie her feet to cycle peddles hoping she would make some effort. But she would fall down. People would advise them different medications, therapies, and even pujas. Divya's parents would try them all, hoping for a miracle. The doctors told them that Divya's physiotherapy sessions should become a part of their daily regime. Her parents could forget to go to temple for a day, but never skipped her therapy sessions. They knew that if they did not make the sessions a religion, Divya's condition would only worsen.

It was not just Divya's medical condition that her parents had to deal with. Despite living in Delhi where there are plenty of 'good' schools, her parents had a tough time getting her admitted into one. None of the 'big' schools was willing to accept her. Finally, they reluctantly enrolled Divya into a school in their locality, which was willing to give her admission. The school did not have much to speak of in terms of amenities but Divya's parents did not have a choice.

Despite all the obstacles, her parents ensured a happy childhood for Divya. Divya recalls her childhood to be a wonderful and positive one,

"I was a very cheerful child. The best part was that at home, I was never treated differently. I loved to study and engrossed myself in my books."

Divya's first stint with Bollywood happened when she was picked as a child actor for a Jackie Shroff film. The movie was called *Shiva ka Insaaf*. The crew needed small children for a song. Divya's mother vividly remembers how Jackie Shroff himself lifted Divya from her wheelchair and carried her to the shoot. The shooting continued for ten days. After ten days, a unit member told her how her daughter had all the qualities of being a star and advised her to get Divya to Mumbai where he would launch her as a child artist. When Divya's mother showed no interest, the unit member remarked,

"ये लड़की हमारे लिए ही बनी है, आप देखिएगा"
(This girl is destined for Bollywood; you just wait and watch).

While Divya's mother left the conversation at that, it was etched in Divya's heart and she would never forget it. Years later, Divya was indeed to become a known name in the Indian film industry.

When Divya's sister was born, Divya resolved that her sister would never suffer any discrimination because of her. Her mother wanted to admit her sister in the same school. But Divya knew her sister's potential would be wasted as the school did not have many facilities. So she asked her mother to admit her to a school with better amenities. However, when the school authorities came to know of this, they felt they had been insulted. They threw Divya out of the school. The irony of the whole thing was that the school principal herself had polio. How could she then have been so apathetic?

Divya got admission in a school run by the Spastic Society, an NGO dedicated to the welfare of people with neuro-muscular disorders. But she was never happy studying in a special school.

> *"We do not need special schools. In fact, if everything is given to you, you stop making progress. All we need is some special infrastructural support in the same schools where other children go. We should not be isolated in our own world. How else can we ever be an integral part of the same society?"*

It was at this school that Divya met a teacher, Ms Beera Mitra, who has been her role model and inspiration. She showed a lot of confidence in Divya when others did not see her potential.

> *"She told me, 'Divya, you will not let me down.' Even today, whatever I do in life, I always tell myself I cannot let her down. That makes me give my 100 percent to it."*

Divya is still in touch with her teacher and calls her on all important occasions to seek her blessings. Theirs is truly an amazing student-teacher bond.

After her class X, Divya withdrew from the Spastic school and started studying through distance education. But she never lost her focus and always set herself high goals. Divya wanted to get into Delhi University's best college and for that, she put all her efforts. Her dedication and perseverance finally bore fruit.

Divya got admission into Lady Shri Ram College in New Delhi. The college is well known worldwide and needs no introduction. She completed her double MA in Sociology, World Cinema and a French language course from Paris. When asked how she managed it all, she makes it seem so simple;

"Like everyone else does."

Divya is a bundle of positive attitude and optimism. She decided early in her childhood that she wanted to live like a normal person. Divya would never pity herself, nor would she let anyone else do so.

LSR extended Divya support in all possible ways. The faculty, the administration, Divya's friend circle, everyone was supportive in making it easy for her. She was even allowed to be accompanied by a full-time maid.

"I am a high headed snobbish LSRian and love to boast about my college."

What the unit member had told her mother in her childhood had stayed with Divya. But she was shy and had stage fright. Even in the Spastic Society school assemblies, she could never perform on stage. Divya wanted to be an actor but did not know how to overcome her stage fright. It was only in LSR that Divya discovered her true potential. She involved herself with a street theatre group where she worked with some of the best of actors in Delhi. Through her plays, she worked on various social issues. Her plays were about being socially responsible and about spreading awareness about various social evils. She always tried to find a purpose in everything she did.

From a shy girl to a national award winner (Divya has won the President's award for entertainment as an actor, writer and director), the journey has been an exciting one for Divya.

Meanwhile, Divya also started writing film critiques. When the movie *Black* was released, Divya hated the whole treatment of the concept of blindness and wrote to Sanjay Leela Bansali expressing her concerns and reservations about the movie. The way the characters behaved with the little girl was totally against her philosophies. By then, owing to her plays she had come to be known as a social activist. Sanjay appreciated her views and met Divya to allay her concerns. The meeting lasted for four hours and they kept in touch from there on.

Divya got her big break when Sanjay Leela Bhansali decided to make *Guzaarish* and Divya was called in to train Hrithik Roshan. Ever since then, Divya has not looked back on her journey of life.

"Although I was born in Delhi, Mumbai is my 'final destination'. I hope to die in the arms of the ocean."

Her parents were obviously concerned for their daughter. They were reluctant at first but their daughter's determination softened their stance. Initially, Divya stayed in a guest house of the Spastic Society and that eased her parents' worry. Later, when they finally understood that Divya had gone to stay for a long time, her parents went over and settled her in a rented flat in Mumbai. Divya's full time maid from Delhi went to stay with her. She has always been an important part of Divya's life.

"She is my hands, my strength. She too loves me with all her heart and soul. She is a family member to me."

Divya calls herself a global citizen. Her father had a lot of foreign assignments and they would frequently travel to Europe, the UK, the US and Paris. Divya can speak six languages – Hindi, English, French, Japanese, Nepali and a little bit of Marathi. She is a connoisseur of wines and loves indulging in French wines.

> *"In all these countries, there were a lot of facilities for disabled people. But when we would come to India, I would see the way our country was agnostic to the needs of differently-abled people. People are insensitive out here. Unless it happens to any of your family members, you couldn't care less."*

On her list of other achievements, Divya is a panel member of the Indian Council for Cultural Relations. She runs her own NGO called 'Ahead' which is working on creating awareness on social issues. Ahead has directed more than twenty-five plays on different social issues. Her adaption of a foreign play 'The Melody of Love' has been performed more than fifty times.

We have often heard non-disabled people felicitating disabled people for their achievements. But in a first, Divya organised a unique event called 'Boundless 2012' to felicitate non-disabled people who, through their contributions, made a positive difference to the community of the disabled.

At present, Divya is the Creative Associate with Cineyug Entertainment Pvt Ltd in Mumbai, the full time job that has provided her the outlet to her innate creativity and has given her the wings of independence as a young independent woman. With all her experience in the field of entertainment and Bollywood, Divya along with a close friend has also launched Cineaddicts, a home production house. Divya is now ready to present her maiden independent Bollywood Romantic Comedy feature film *Pyaar Actually*. Divya always does things big, and once again the film will be world's first feature film to be written, directed and made by a wheelchair-bound film-maker. She will also be seen acting alongside many Bollywood superstars. Apart from the commercial angle, the film will also felicitate opportunities for special talent that some or most 'normal' people consider unworthy with the hope of making a positive difference to the community of the disabled.

Recently, in a one of its kind, India hosted its first beauty pageant with a difference – Miss Wheelchair India. It was conceived to provide a platform for aspiring beauties on wheelchairs to make a foray into the field of fashion, television, etc. Needless to say, our very own Divya not only participated, but was also the first runner up of the event.

When one of the judges asked Divya what would she do if she had only a week to live, Divya's reply was,

"I would do something which will inspire others like me to come out of their shells and fly high."

Divya feels being adjudged Ms. India runner-up is a big responsibility. After winning the title, she does not want to sit in one corner and bask in the glory of the same but go out and conquer the world. Her mission in life is to keep striving for the next level. As she says,

"After all these little milestones, I feel I am some worth in this big universe."

You definitely are, Divya!

Divya gets a little pensive when I ask her what her future plans are. After a pause she says,

> *"I have the same hopes from life as you have. I feel the same emotions. I would also love to enjoy watching a sunset in the arms of someone special. Yashji once said, 'There is someone for everyone.' Sooner or later, I will meet him. And then, like every woman, I would fall in love."*

Divya's smile leaves me hopeful. I hope she meets her man soon. I wish her professional and personal success. Above all, I fold my hands and make a *guzaarish* to God for a healthy life for this young lady whose spirit is unconquerable and charm unstoppable.

Divya can be reached at divya1406@gmail.com.

Disability and Recreation

Amidst all the discussions about unemployment, poverty and attitudinal issues, recreation might seem to be a trivial thing to be discussed in this book. Nevertheless, what is also a fact is that human beings cannot work for 24 hours a day and they spend a considerable amount of time in watching television, reading books, enjoying sport and other such activities. Though, all this is very much taken for granted by the likes of you and me, when it comes to disabled people, even such things seem to be a luxury.

How can a visually-impaired person enjoy a television serial when he cannot appreciate what is being said through the visual emotions of the characters? How can he read the same books, newspapers and magazines which we read on a daily basis? Audio books are a blessing in disguise but the question of affordability and availability remains. *My Name is Khan*, a Hindi movie starring Shahrukh Khan was the first movie to be made for visually handicapped people. It contained in depth narration of what was happening on the screen, different emotions and even special background sets and colours. Such efforts should be made by all big theatres and production houses in the country.

A hearing-impaired person cannot make out what dialogues are being exchanged by the characters on the show. Why can't every show have sub-titles so that even the deaf community can sit and enjoy shows?

When it comes to sports, George's concept of blind cricket and Prakash's, Vinod's and Major Singh's miraculous feats have left me thinking how and why I had never earlier associated sports with disability. These men have changed my attitude towards sports. They have proven that the right infrastructure is all it takes. And then, the sky is the limit. Today I know many men and women who have brought laurels for the country in the Paralympics; only that they never find mention in mainstream media. It is sad that even differently-abled people are not aware that something called Paralympics exists on national and international levels. Prakash's revelations on how the infrastructure in our country curtails rather than promote sports for disabled people are shocking and need urgent attention of the sports ministry.

Even shopping malls, restaurants, parking spaces and other public places like parks need to be made disabled friendly both in terms of accessibility and sensitisation of the people working there.

All this will not just give India a social and economic advantage but will place it among world's best tourist countries. A beginning has been made. Let's make life more cheerful for the differently-abled.

Prakash Nadar:
Free Willy

Bounded by crutches;
Water set me free.
It was when I threw away my limitations;
I truly became a free Willy.

In the '70s, lack of awareness and inaccessibility of vaccination cost many people their ability to move. Polio had become a silent killer. Among many such unfortunate children was a child named Prakash whose parents casually 'forgot' to get him vaccinated against polio. This casual mistake proved disastrous for their little one. Polio-afflicted Prakash became a social stigma. Young Prakash found himself alone and made friends with the flowing water body behind his house. The murky gutter waters flowing into the Arabian Sea became his best friend. Like a true friend, it gifted him what no one else could – self-confidence and pride. Thirty-five years later, like free Willy, Prakash broke free from his wheelchair and crutches and surrendered to his friend. The longest swimathon in the history of open water swimming and a world record – Prakash's achievements come from meagre resources and lack of support. His story is an important lesson

*Prakash threw away his crutches and embraced waters as a swimmer.
He found a place in Limca Book of Records after swimming
underwater for 42 Kms from Mumbai to Raigad and
back in record time.*

of how sports can be used to uplift the differently-abled and give them new wings.

An individual haul of over one hundred and twenty medals in several national and international sports competitions in just over ten years is no ordinary feat. What makes this achievement even more outstanding is the fact that it is an achievement of a person whom many of us would otherwise have sympathised with if we were to see him on the streets. It is the achievement of thirty-five-year-old polio afflicted man, Prakash Nadar.

Being the youngest child of his parents, one would have expected that Prakash's parents would have been experienced enough to get their newly born a polio dose without fail. But lack of awareness made them casual. Little did they know how it would affect their child's future.

At one-and-a-half years of age, Prakash had very high fever and his legs became paralysed. He was brought to a nearby hospital where doctors diagnosed him with polio. His father ran a general store. With three other children to take care of, Prakash's disability was not only emotionally traumatic for his family but also a big financial burden.

His parents got him admitted in a school for differently-abled children. Thereafter, Prakash underwent treatment for the next nine years. Even after the treatment, he could walk only with the help of crutches. The frequent trips to the hospitals meant that Prakash had to miss a lot of classes. Overwhelmed with pain and self-pity, studying was the last thing on his mind. But Prakash's lack of interest in studies was compensated by his interest in sports.

Prakash's house was in Worli in Mumbai, very close to the Arabian Sea. Whenever he had time, he would go and sit near the sea behind his house. He would sit there for hours at a stretch, gazing at the open waters. He would see people freely swimming in the open waters. The longing for freedom inculcated in him a love for water and a longing to explore the waters. Prakash decided to learn swimming.

When he first shared his desire of swimming with his family, they were both irritated and tense. How could a boy who could not even walk develop such an absurd interest? Moreover, the water in that area had claimed many lives. Prakash could not even afford to pay the fees of a professional swimming trainer. His parents were justified in their concerns for his safety and dissuaded him. But then, Prakash was only a child. How could he forego his new found companionship with the waters?

His friend, Selva Kumar would literally carry him to the sea and throw him in the waters. Swimming was all about control over the body and breath. Prakash could not move his legs so he swam with his hands. He learnt freestyle and backstroke too. He soon learnt that despite his inability to walk, he could float freely in water. Being in water made him free.

Prakash's self-training made him popular among his friends. He started winning many swimming competitions in school. It was during one such event that Prakash met the legendary Rajaram Ghag, the second handicapped person in the world to have swum across the English Channel. Rajaram became a role model for Prakash who was around thirteen years old at that time. All these years, he had always felt his life was of no use. But meeting Rajaram changed his outlook and gave him a lot of positive energy. Prakash also began to think that he too could do something worthwhile in his life. With swimming, he found acceptance. Prakash realised if he had to carve out an identity for himself, it had to be through sports. From his disability, he started focussing on his abilities.

But as is said, the day you realise what you wish to do, life starts testing your determination, before showing you the way.

The special school where he was studying had classes till fourth standard only. Soon it was time for Prakash to move to a new school. In his first school, there were less than twenty children per class. The kind of attention that was paid to each individual student was enormous. But in the new school, there were more than a hundred students in one class and Prakash was the only disabled student. He suddenly felt lost. His interest and involvement in sports were gone. The school provided no special facilities, assistance or encouragement in any manner.

Prakash continued his swimming practice after school hours. Unable to cope up with the new environment in school, Prakash finally left studies.

Prakash knew that beyond this point in life, it was only sports that could take him further. He started actively looking out for competitions in which physically handicapped people could participate. But there were very few of those. Prakash decided not to restrict himself to swimming but instead try to master other sports as well. He started participating in several other sports like badminton, lawn tennis and weight lifting. Each event he participated in helped him build a further network of friends and get to know about similar competitions on bigger and larger platforms.

In 1997, Prakash participated in his first ever national level athletics championship and won a gold medal. This gave him immense confidence.

At a national swimming competition in Gwalior, Prakash won a silver medal even though he had participated without any formal coaching. It was there that he was noticed by a doctor who was impressed by Prakash's will and courage. The doctor agreed to help Prakash and arranged passes for him to practice in a swimming pool near his house. Prakash's joy knew no bounds.

In another such competition, he was noticed by Balasaheb Gadge, now an assistant commissioner of police. Gadge offered to pay for Prakash's swimming training in the police camp in Worli. With proper training, Prakash won many national competitions and was adjudged the best Indian swimmer in the handicapped category.

In the interim, Prakash got married to Satya. The couple has been blessed with two children: son Hariharan and daughter Varshini.

"My family, including my children, has been my biggest support. After their birth, I have a greater share of responsibilities on my shoulders and I wish I can make them proud of their father."

In 2002, Prakash was selected to represent the country in the Asian Games.

He went there, determined to do his best. But reality hit him hard when he met sportspersons from other countries. Globally, disabled sportspersons receive tremendous support from their respective sports ministries. Be it training facilities, medical or financial support, countries make it easier for their players to focus on sports and bring laurels to their countries.

"In India, even the abled players do not receive that much support; leave aside differently-abled sportspersons. Indian players have very strong willpower which keeps them going."

Prakash could not win a medal at the Asian Games. But he came back with a more determined attitude to work towards the cause of sports, especially for the disabled people in the country. Sports had transformed his life and had changed the attitude of society towards him. Prakash wanted to help others like him to move ahead.

Prakash adds,

"I want to tell the government that it always announces cash awards for an athlete when he or she wins a medal. In fact, there should be monetary help before the games. That money will help in preparations and help us to give our best at the games."

At this juncture, a pertinent question comes to my mind. Why not involve disabled people in the policy making decisions in the field of sports? After all, wouldn't they be able to bring out the real difficulties and suggest practical solutions?

After the Asian Games, Prakash got involved in several social activities, helping other disabled people fulfil their dreams in the field of sports. He participated in a motorbike rally from Kanyakumari to Kashmir, trying to raise awareness among people towards the cause of disability. He has worked with several NGOs and has organised several medical camps for the disabled people. Prakash has donated blood for more than sixty times in life. He has even employed four physically-challenged people at his general store.

Prakash had long wanted to do something unprecedented in the history of sports. After giving it a deep and determined thought, he decided to swim across a forty-two-kilometre stretch of the Arabian Sea. Prakash was supported in his endeavour by Nitesh Rane, son of a prominent Congress leader and leader of Swabhiman Sanghatana, an NGO for the poor in the state of Maharashtra. Rane, along with V Mahalingam, Income Tax Commissioner, helped Prakash undergo rigorous training to achieve his dream.

The task was formidable. No one had attempted it before and the risks involved were huge. But Prakash had stopped fearing the waters and had befriended them instead. So he began preparing mentally and physically for this challenging task. He was coached by Shekhar Damodar Surve. Prakash found not just supporters but dissuaders as well. Many told him he was playing with his life. But for Prakash, the only thing on his mind was to make a record. Prakash knew his record could help bring recognition for other disabled sportspersons and would open new frontiers for them.

After months of practice, Prakash chose 8 March for his swimathon. It is celebrated as International Women's Day and he wanted to pay a tribute to the women in the society, especially his mother.

"Women, especially from a certain strata in society, face huge challenges. In a way, they may be as handicapped as people like us. Through my attempt, I wanted to give them the courage to break those barriers."

On 8 March 2013, at noon, flanked by his family, friends, well wishers and the media, Prakash entered the waters from the Gateway of India. Two boats followed him, recording his expedition and supporting him. His coach was in one of the boats. Over the next eighteen hours, Prakash swam relentlessly. He reached his destination, Rewas in Raigad in the Arabian Sea and without halting, swam back to the Gateway of India at 6 am the next day.

Prakash had just set a world record and his name was registered in the Limca Book of Records!

*"It was frightening at many moments. It was the first time
I had been in water overnight. I had to fight big fishes and
tidal waves to complete my record. In fact, when I came
out I could not believe I had made it. I cried in happiness."*

National and international media covered this impossible feat. Prakash had just registered his name in the history of sports. At that moment, Prakash found the meaning of his life. At that moment, nobody looked down upon him. At that moment, the eyes around him were full of pride and not sympathy. At that moment, Prakash had changed society's attitude towards the differently-abled. At that moment, Prakash was free!

*"I wanted to prove that every person can break out of his or
her limitations."*

Despite such impossible feats, Prakash's struggles continue. The Indian government has not done much to help Prakash scale newer heights. Beyond some coverage in papers and recognition seminars, they seem to have conveniently forgotten him.

I sincerely wish policy makers would wake up to help people like Prakash who light up the darkness in their world through their hard work and undefeatable spirit.

Prakash can be contacted at prakashmnadar76@gmail.com.

Major DP Singh:
Bhaag DP Bhaag

It is said in life everything has a purpose;
Even the difficult moments and adversities.
I am not here to brood over life's challenges;
I would rather treat them as opportunities.

The Kargil War almost killed him. With fifty shrapnel piercing his body and body weight of just 28 kgs, he was declared dead. It is truly a miracle that Major DP Singh is running miles on his prosthetic limb today. A near death experience has made this man all the more fearless. From being suddenly physically challenged to making challengers out of other disabled people, the fighter in him has not just kept him afloat but has also challenged his own physical limitations. His story is all about finding a mission – a purpose in life. Meet the real Indian soldier in this story.

Devender Pal Singh's father worked in the Border Roads Organisation and had a transferrable job. DP spent early years of his childhood with his grandparents in Roorkee. Staying with his grandparents and in proximity to a gurudwara had a profound impact on the young mind. The gurudwara near their house recited the *Guru Granth Sahib* in an easy and understandable

From a soldier mortally wounded in the Kargil war to a marathon runner, Major DP Singh has come a long way. His never say die spirit inspires many and that keeps him running, literally too.

language. This inculcated in him a great sense of connectedness to the Sikh religion. As a young child, DP deeply imbibed the sacred values of the Sikh religion: values of sacrifice, of placing the country before self, of martyrdom and of detachment. Even from the movies he watched, he consciously tried to see what qualities did the hero's character signify so that he could inculcate some of those. He studied in a Kendriya Vidyalaya close to an Army base camp and maintained by the India Army. So, it was no surprise that DP Singh grew up with the dream of joining the Indian Army.

In a place like Roorkee, where children eat, dream and sleep the IIT engineering entrance, DP did not even fill the forms. Wearing the green uniform became his mission in life. His family was supportive of their child's ambition and dream and did not pressurise him to do something he did not want to.

When DP did not clear the NDA exam after Class XII, he was dejected but did not feel defeated. The next option to enter the Army was to attempt the CDS (Combined Defence Services) exam after graduation. He had to pick a stream for his graduation. DP decided to challenge his own shortcomings and picked a stream in which he was weak – accounts. He got through the bank recruitment exam and started working part time, pursuing his graduation through correspondence. His dream of joining the Indian Army remained at the back of his mind.

After he completed his graduation, DP gave the CDS exam a shot and was selected. With great pride, he joined the Indian Military Academy (IMA) in the year 1995. After a year-and-a-half long training, in December 1997, DP was formally commissioned to the Indian Army (an occasion when the President of India confers the officer rank on successful completion of Army training).

He was elated to join the Dogra regiment in the Infantry division. Infantry was his first love. No sooner had he completed his training and joined the battalion, the Kargil war shook the nation. He was sent straight to the battleground to lead his team of twenty-eight men. Operation Vijay was in full swing.

Speaking about his thoughts at that time, DP says,

"For every soldier, it is a dream to fight and die for one's country. The Army trains you to take pride in sacrificing for the motherland. As a person we all know that wars are futile and do not yield any good results. But as a soldier, it is our duty to protect our motherland. We have to kill the enemy or else they will kill us. Contrary to what you might think, soldiers do not have any second thoughts about putting their lives at risk. For them, it is their duty, their job. Nobody thinks twice and nobody repents."

Destiny had its own plans for DP. The day of 15 July 1999 is etched in the Major's memories. After a lull of forty-eight hours, Major DP's post was attacked again. Before he knew, a bomb landed next to him and disintegrated into hundreds of shrapnels. Fifty shrapnels pierced through his body. Within fractions of a second, blood gushed out from minute holes in his body. He was bleeding profusely and was carried to the medical camp across a river channel where he was administered first aid. Even the nearest hospital was not so near and took the team two-and-a-half hours to reach. DP was declared dead on arrival. The story of a brave soldier could have ended there...

But as is an old saying, "जाको राखे साईयाँ, मार सके न कोय" *(He who is protected by God cannot be killed).*

It must have been by God's will that a senior anaesthetic arrived at the hospital on an unplanned visit. An expert at reviving people, he took a shot and DP survived. DP was in coma for two days. Gangrene, a potentially life threatening condition that arises when a considerable mass of body tissue dies, had infected his toe. DP was moved to a bigger hospital in Udhampur. When DP regained consciousness and looked at his leg, he instantly knew there was no option but amputation. The infection was spreading fast and if his leg was not amputated soon, the infection would spread throughout his body.

> "Even before the doctor told me, I knew about the amputation. On the third day, when they opened my band-aid, I saw that nothing was left in that part of my leg. The doctor was hesitant in telling me the inevitable. When he told me about the amputation, I told him to go ahead and operate without any hesitation. I was not negative about it. Even my first reaction was not of denial but acceptance of it as God's wish. I thought to myself that it would be a new challenge to lead the life of a physically challenged person.
>
> "Lying in the hospital's ICU and declared dangerously ill, I found a chanting wheel (a symbol of positivity in Buddhism) in the hospital bedside table. I knew it was not by mere coincidence it was kept there. It was there to protect me from evil. It was there to give me God's message."

DP's leg was amputated and he was put under observation. But a continuous high fever of 104-105 degrees and incessant vomiting worried his doctors. Soon he was moved to Delhi where he underwent a second stomach operation to remove a damaged intestinal part.

It was after several surgeries that DP was finally able to stand with the help of crutches. Army doctors referred his case to an artificial limb centre in Pune. When he reached Pune, the doctors were shocked to know that DP had travelled by train. People in his medical condition were always transported by air.

To the doctors' utter dismay, DP weighed just 28 kgs! DP was clearly not fit enough to be fitted with an artificial limb. He had to stay in the hospital for close to a year before moving out on an artificial limb. During this one year, he was in the company of several other soldiers who had been critically injured in the war.

> "We did not let each other feel as if we were in a hospital. We behaved as if we were friends on a vacation, staying together, recovering, relaxing and enjoying. The Army takes good care of its soldiers."

Barely two days after reaching Pune, DP asked his parents to go back home. He assured them that he would take good care of himself. He did not want them to be with him in the hospital doing nothing.

> "Idleness would have led to mental stress for them. Seeing me at peace with myself even on the first day of my consciousness from coma was assuring for them."

His courage and fighting spirit are truly overwhelming. Fifty shrapnels had impregnated the body of this man and are still inside him. As I sit in front of a man who survived death and listen to this miraculous story, I am speechless. For the first time, I understand the meaning of fearlessness. Name a body part and DP can tell you what medical issues it can have. He fights these day-in and day-out and yet he never lets them grow on him. Sometimes the shrapnel hurt and DP feels the pain in his limbs but the manner in which he has accepted it all leaves me wondering how strong a man he is. He shares the secret of his spirit,

> *"You must be wondering how I survived and how I move and run. The human body is a beautiful thing, my friend. It is the mind which should control the body. But when we get sick or ill, it is our body which takes over our mind. It is a combination of my religious upbringing and Army training which has helped me sail through. Or else I would probably have just been another war-injured forgotten soldier."*

Soon after moving out of the hospital, DP was stationed in Pune for a year-and-a-half. The regret remained that he would not find a posting in the infantry again and he would be restricted strictly to administrative tasks.

DP had to begin life anew. Like a child, he had to learn balancing on an artificial limb and walking without support. He had to get into the habit of controlling his weight. A loss of an inch rendered his prosthetic limb loose and vice versa. Despite the doctors handing him a list of precautions, DP decided to listen to his own willpower and put life back on track as it had always been. After all, at one point of time, medical science had even declared him dead. DP wanted to challenge his own self to uncover new opportunities. He puts it in very beautiful words when he says,

> *"Thanks to those who critiqued me and doubted me that I have developed the spirit to fight and improve. Thanks to medical science which declared me dead that my faith in God has became stronger."*

In the year 2000, DP got married and in 2002, he was blessed with a son. His wife and son carry the same positive attitude as him.

In the army, sports had been an important part of his routine. DP again started engaging in sports. Initially sceptical, DP started with golf and soon graduated to squash. Speaking about his love for sports, DP says,

> *"One hour of a game can teach some of the best lessons of life – team spirit, leadership, and winning spirit."*

DP refers to the famous proverb,

> *"The Battle of Waterloo was won on the playing fields of Eton" (referring to the fighting spirit of the soldiers induced in them by sports and games).*

In 2005, Army organised a car rally from Kargil to Kanyakumari to commensurate the heroes and martyrs of Kargil war. DP participated in the same and found an instant passion for rally sports. Despite his enthusiastic participation in this rally, DP found no takers to sponsor him in subsequent rallies. Most people he met felt he was incapable of driving such a long distance. That came as a huge shock for DP. Despite proving himself time and again, DP did not get any support. He knew he had to do something remarkably different to prove his capabilities to the world.

It was in the month of October 2009 that DP saw an advertisement in the newspaper about the Airtel Delhi Half Marathon. The marathon was forty days away. He was quick to see an opportunity and enrolled for the same. The very next morning, DP wore his jogging suit, went out on road and started with a normal walk. He walked for about 2 kilometres. But preparing for the marathon was easier said than done.

DP did not know how to run on a prosthetic limb. He had lost the stamina and endurance to run. When he would run fast or for long period, his prosthetic limb would not support him and would start bleeding. His stomach had undergone laparotomy twice and the going was tough.

But DP was not to be defeated. He researched and got to know about the running legend Terry Fox. Terrance Stanley 'Terry' Fox was a Canadian athlete, humanitarian, and cancer research activist. In 1980, his one leg had been amputated and yet he had embarked on a cross-Canada run to raise money and awareness for cancer research. Although the spread of his cancer eventually forced him to end his quest after 143 days and 5,373 kilometres (3,339 miles), and ultimately cost him his life, his efforts resulted in a lasting worldwide legacy.

> "I tried the hop/skip style of running, where you jump twice on the good foot and then land on the prosthetic foot and repeat. This got me moving a bit faster. My own leg had to learn how to run alongside a mechanical leg which was quite alien to it and a lot of the practice was needed to train my brain."

In his practice sessions over the next twenty days, DP could run up to a maximum of nine kilometres a day. On the day of the half marathon, he had to run twenty-one kilometres. Sceptical eyes greeted him. Many times he felt he could not go on any longer. Giving up would have been the easiest option for anyone in his place, but not for the Army Major. When he was running, he was not competing against anyone else, but his own shortcomings.

He completed the run in 3 hours and 40 minutes. Touching the finish line was one of the happiest moments of his life. The sweat and the adrenaline rush made him ecstatic. DP smiles and shares one of the most precious moments of the day,

"As I was crossing Rajpath, a spectator on a wheelchair waived at me and smiled. I felt as if my run had motivated that person. I recollected my first thought after getting injured. Perhaps through me God wanted to send a message to physically challenged people; a message of determination, message of courage, message of perseverance. It was as if in that one moment, I had found the purpose of my existence."

Major DP Singh's name was listed in the Limca Book of Records for being the first Indian who ran a half marathon despite being physically handicapped.

In the year 2011, Army gave him a specialised blade for running. Made from several layers of carbon fibre, each layer thinner than a human hair, the blade is a specialised equipment that stores kinetic energy from the wearer's steps as potential energy. Like a spring, it allows the wearer to run and jump. It has been frequently used by athletes across the world as its mechanics allow one to run just as fast as any other runner. Running on the blade was a new challenge for DP as he had to unlearn running on the prosthetic limb and learn running on the new blade.

Since then, there has been no stopping for the Major. He has run more than ten half marathons. Every time he runs, he sets a target of improving his own timing and each time he conquers his limitations and betters his own records by fifteen minutes. His current timing stands at two hours and ten minutes.

He has achieved all of this after a lot of practice. The Major follows a religious regime of waking up at 4 am and practicing three hours a day without fail. There have been occasions when his body resists and he is in pain for days. There have been occasions when the doctor had advised him bed rest but the Major would run. He knew that if he didn't, it would de-motivate the other physically challenged runners who have joined him over a period of time.

Major DP Singh hopes to be running full marathons soon. Just some years ago, India had no one like DP, but today, there are close to fifteen such athletes running in the country, motivated and inspired by DP's courage and never say die spirit.

Leave aside other people, even the differently-abled people in the country are not aware of dedicated sports events in the handicapped category. DP's endeavour is to create awareness and instil confidence in many more disabled people so they can find their strength and fighting spirit by engaging in sports.

DP is currently working as a manager in a private bank. He has started a social media drive through his group called, 'The Challenging Ones'. The group works as a peer support group for physically disabled people and their families. The idea is to spread awareness, motivate parents of disabled children, develop a positive attitude in them and bring out leaders through the medium of sports. Every time a physically handicapped runs on the road showing his prosthetic limb, more people open up and think of making a beginning.

DP says that at the end of the day it is the thoughts of a disabled person which can truly determine his destiny. He gives a very simple and yet a powerful example when he says,

"One of the biggest challenges of a prosthetic limb is sweat. When you sweat, the prosthetic sockets trap sweat and

prevent air from circulating around your residual limb, which can create a virtual paradise for bacteria. Bacterial and fungal infections can lead to skin irritation, abrasions and eventually skin breakdown.

"Now imagine a person living in Mumbai or Chennai. The weather there is such that one cannot help sweating. So what does one do? Does one simply run away from one's hometown? Or does one adapt by simply beginning to take the necessary care of the limb?

"Being physically challenged is a lot about one's attitude. The rest can be conquered."

DP ends the conversation with the following words,

"Everything in life has a purpose. Sometimes the answers come quick; sometimes they take a little longer. The most difficult times are God's way of teaching us, mentoring us. God is the greatest teacher and I am his humble disciple. I pray he never leaves his disciple till he makes him perfect and pure."

Major DP Singh can be contacted at majordpsingh@gmail.com.

Concluding Remarks

There are many more people whose stories I would have liked to include in the book. For the sake of brevity, I could not. Nevertheless, their names deserve a special mention here.

The story of Shubh Kaur Ghumman, India's one legged dancer has touched a million hearts. Her eyes speak volumes about her undying passion for life. Her smile carries the many dreams of a quintessential Indian girl.

Major HPS Ahluwalia suffered a bullet injury in the 1965 Indo-Pak war. After struggling for two years, he realised there was a lack of adequate medical facilities in the country and he set up the Indian Spinal Injuries Centre in New Delhi. Today, the Indian Spinal Injuries Centre is a landmark healthcare institute at par with the best in the world.

Arunima Sinha, a former national-level volleyball player was shoved from a moving train by thieves when she reportedly attempted to fight them off as they tried to steal her purse. Two years later, she became the first female amputee to climb Mount Everest. She proved to the world that a disabled person was not an object of pity.

Malathi Krishnamurthy Holla is an International para-athlete from India. Born into a poor family, a raging fever paralysed Malathi's entire body when she was just a year old. Electric shock treatment for more than two years saw little Malathi regaining strength in her upper body, but her lower body remained completely weak. Notwithstanding the trials and turbulences that plagued her, Malathi chose sports as the best alternative medicine to forget her pain, and went on to become one of the most inspiring sports personalities of modern India. With over three hundred medals in her kitty, Malathi was conferred the prestigious Arjuna and Padma Shri Awards. Malathi shelters children with various disabilities at the Mathru Foundation – a charitable trust she founded along with her friends.

There are many more achievers like the ones above, people whose stories gave me goose bumps. My journey of interviewing the people in this book has been the greatest learning experience of my life. The meaning of the words 'possible', 'fearlessness', 'hope', 'faith', 'self-belief' and 'life' stand altered in my dictionary ever since I met these men and women. Their fighting spirit, courage, determination, optimism and above all, respect for their own achievements and taking responsibilities of their own destiny is an example for society. These people are not handicapped, but it is our thinking which makes them handicapped. If anything needs to change, it is you and me.